Setting
People
Free

LEADERS GUIDE

Setting People Free

LEADERS GUIDE

DAVID DEVENISH

KINGSWAY PUBLICATIONS
EASTBOURNE

ISBN 1 84291 010 8

Published by
KINGSWAY PUBLICATIONS
Lottbridge Drove, Eastbourne, BN23 6NT, England.
Email: books@kingsway.co.uk

Designed and produced for the publishers by
Bookprint Creative Services, P.O. Box 827, BN21 3YJ, England.
Printed in Great Britain.

Setting People Free

COURSE SYLLABUS

Introduction

Background to the course

In the 1980s, as a pastor of a church in Bedford, England, I found that a substantial amount of my ministry involved seeking to set Christians free from bondages that had held them for many years. These bondages effectively prevented Christians from practical enjoyment of the benefits of their freedom in Christ. These bondages could arise from a number of different causes such as:

● Past sins in a person's life, which still influenced their thought patterns and emotions.

● Emotional pain and hurts as a result of serious sins committed against them, or past trauma from which they did not appear to be able to walk free.

● Lack of understanding of the blessings of their freedom in Christ and their acceptance through God's grace.

● Demonic power that still held them in its grip and which they had neither been set free from nor learned how to fight.

Furthermore, as the Holy Spirit began to move more powerfully in the church and we began to open ourselves up to the tangible presence of God, we found that more of these issues came to the surface. At one time, I actually started to pray that God would bring out issues in people's lives that limited them from making progress in their Christian faith.

We also saw a number of people converted from backgrounds of major emotional damage and we needed to find biblical ways of setting such people free and helping them forward in a life of discipleship.

As I found myself ministering to many people in such circumstances, I soon realised that it was essential to train others in our church to undertake this sort of ministry. I did this in two ways:

- By having them alongside me in ministry situations so that they could learn practically 'on the job'.

- By preparing a caring and healing course to equip them to understand the biblical values, methodology and skills necessary for this sort of ministry.

I first taught the course to a small group in my church, expecting that would be the end of it. Unexpectedly, as far as I was concerned, God seemed to own the course and as a result I have now taught it over 50 times, primarily in this nation but in other countries as well.

Duration and shape of the course

The course is divided into seven sessions, each of which normally takes between one hour and one-and-a-half hours to teach. However, taking questions or doing group work can lengthen the time of each session or of the course as a whole, and it can be adapted accordingly. It can be taught over a single weekend or over seven weeks, one evening per week.

We believe not only in giving information, but also in the impartation of spiritual gifts. The experience of the power of dynamic spiritual resources necessary for involvement in this sort of ministry is an important component of the course. When taking the course, therefore, it is important also to lay on hands and pray for the participants, that God would equip them to be able to minister prayerfully, sensitively and biblically to others. When I take the course, I always have a 'ministry team' with me, and it may be necessary to train such a ministry team first unless they are already well equipped to serve in this capacity.

Also, as the word of God is taught and the Holy Spirit moves during the course, issues in the lives of those participating can sometimes be revealed, so that participants themselves may need biblical counselling and prayer ministry. Sometimes this can be done by the ministry team there and then, but at other times further help is needed. This is why it is essential that this course is taught in a context where ongoing help can be provided. Often we find that others being trained on the same course can, with appropriate instruction and oversight, help those who need ongoing care in relation to issues that may have been revealed by the course.

Who is this course for?

This course is designed for all Christians who want to help others by bringing them to freedom, giving pastoral care and helping them in a life of discipleship. I have heard of pastors and small group leaders who have benefited from the course, but its application is wider than that and can apply to all caring ministries. It does not claim to be a full guide on Christian counselling and many of the issues are not studied in depth. However, it provides a basic guide for understanding the skills necessary to help people forward in understanding and experiencing their freedom in Christ.

How is this leaders guide to be used?

We would suggest that the material in this guide is worked through beforehand by the person or persons teaching the course and also by others who may be involved in a supporting prayer ministry team. It is important that before the course is taught, the issues raised are debated among those who will be teaching and leading it. The course represents a particular value system and philosophy in relation to Christian counselling, which needs to be thought through beforehand. It is not primarily designed for helping those from outside the Christian community, nor for specialist counselling. It is intended rather to equip members of the church to work in teams to counsel and minister to others. It is important that this philosophy is understood when the course is taught.

Obviously it is anticipated that those teaching the leaders guide will themselves have some experience in this sort of Christian ministry. When I teach the course, I use many illustrations from my own experience, asking permission in certain cases and disguising identities. It is important that those teaching the course are able to make it 'live' by giving examples from their own experience. Questions and discussion are to be encouraged.

The course workbook

This is less comprehensive and basically contains the main headings and a summary of the information in the leaders' guide. It is recommended that those on the course keep a separate journal in which to make notes, although there are blank pages at the back which may be used for this purpose.

Foundations for Biblical Counselling

1 Aims of this course

First, we intend to give a foundation for the ministry of setting people free, which is based on the following factors:

- The application of biblical truths to people's lives, without which there can be no true biblical freedom nor a counselling framework which is wholly Christian.

- The expectation of the Holy Spirit moving in power as we pray for people as well as counsel them. This, too, is essential for Christian counselling.

- The use of caring skills which are consistent with the biblical revelation of the character of God. Some of these caring skills may well be learned in secular contexts and we can appreciate and learn from such insights. They would include, for example, listening skills, how to interact with one another genuinely and productively in a counselling context, and a recognition that God sometimes moves suddenly and quickly in a person's life, while at other times He will work through a longer process in which we need to co-operate with Him to bring freedom.

- The belief that 'counselling' must not be separated from 'discipling' and therefore needs to take place primarily within the context of a local church. Making disciples is our calling as Christians and the appropriate vehicle for such a calling is the local church.

There can be a tendency to emphasise one of these factors to the exclusion of the others. For example, we can sometimes rightly diagnose a problem but use the relevant scriptures in a detached, 'proof-text' way, rather than applying them with the appropriate skills necessary to bring the person to a genuine understanding and ability to apply such scriptural principles to their own problem. On the other hand, we could become so enamoured of particular counselling techniques that we fail to apply the word of God in the power of the Holy Spirit. Some others may rightly love to see the Holy Spirit moving dynamically upon somebody, but they fail to emphasise the need also to apply biblical truths to the situation.

Secondly, since we believe that the local church is the primary context within which Christian counselling should take place, we need to see churches become equipped with people who are trained, open to God and able to move in faith and authority to set people free.

Thirdly, with broader vision, we want to play our part in seeing the whole church of God restored to being a place for the healing of the nations. In this aim we co-operate with the medical and psychiatric skills given by God to mankind. Theologians describe these as part of God's 'common grace', which He has made available to all, regardless of whether or not they have appreciated or responded to the truth of His saving grace. However, we must be careful to discern when such medical or psychiatric practice is contrary to God's word.

These aims are necessary because, as we see more people converted from backgrounds of major emotional damage and from the sins which beset our culture, we need to find biblical ways of helping them. Furthermore, we recognise that many Christians need to be set free themselves before they can be effective in setting others free.

2 Biblical foundation for the counselling and caring ministry

a) We are to continue and express the ministry of Jesus

Jesus is described as the 'Wonderful Counsellor' (Isaiah 9:6). It is important to note that this title is used of Jesus in the context of the extension of God's rule. 'Of the increase of his government and peace there will be no end. He will reign on David's throne and over his *kingdom...*' (Isaiah 9:7). Counselling is not merely so that we can feel better, but rather so that God's will can be done more effectively in our lives.

Jesus came to proclaim freedom for the prisoners and to release the oppressed (Luke 4:18), and showed tremendous compassion towards the crowds. When He saw them as 'harassed and helpless, like sheep without a shepherd' (Matthew 9:36), His response was to call upon His disciples to pray for more workers to be sent out to release the crowds from such bondage, thus demonstrating the kingdom of God. The expression 'kingdom of God' refers to the practical extension of God's rule so that His will is done in all circumstances.

b) There are two biblical words that can be used to describe the counselling ministry

- The Greek word *parakaleo* means to encourage or beseech, to draw alongside or be summoned alongside to help. It has the idea of being on somebody's side, helping them, encouraging them forward. It is something that should be part of the normal practice of church life; indeed we are to 'encourage one another daily' (Hebrews 3:13).

- The second word used in this context has a somewhat different meaning. *Noutheteo* means to admonish, warn or correct. It has the idea of confrontation; of calling for a change in behaviour; of challenging someone to stop acting in a wrong way and start doing what God wants them to do.

These two words held in balance describe Christian counselling well.

Our objective is to bring about changes in people's:

- behaviour
- attitudes
- motives

We are seeking to see people become more Christlike so that the image of God is reflected in them. However, Christian counselling focuses not only on outward behaviour and feelings but upon inner attitudes and motives as well. It is worth pointing out that behaviour will not change permanently without a genuine change of attitude and motivation.

As has already been said, it is open to all of us in the church to serve one another in this way. However, Romans 12:8 makes it clear that encouraging or counselling is also a particular ministry that some people have.

A key scripture is: 'Praise be to the God and Father of our Lord Jesus Christ, the Father of compassion and the God of all comfort, who comforts us in all our troubles, so that we can comfort those in any trouble with the comfort we ourselves have received from God' (2 Corinthians 1:3–4). Why does God comfort us? So that we can comfort others who are in trouble. This is the basis upon which we can help one another. In other words, our receiving help from God is not just to make us feel better, but so that we are equipped to minister to others.

What have we got to give to one another? We minister to others with the comfort we have already received from God. In other words, it is a divine supply of encouragement and comfort, which we minister to others.

c) We are to love one another (John 13:34)

Within the context of the Christian church, counselling should be seen as a caring expression of our love for each other, rather than as a professional/client relationship.

d) We are to carry each other's burdens (Galatians 6:2)

Paul describes this instruction as the 'law of Christ'. Throughout Galatians he is concerned to set his readers free from a merely legalistic observance of Christianity, and in Galatians 6 he gives the characteristics of Christ's attitude, which is also to be the attitude of Christ's people. It is helpful to read through this section – Galatians 6:1–5 – because it gives principles which are very important for counselling ministry. Even when we are counselling people because of their own sins, we are to restore them gently, and recognise that we could also be tempted in the same way. This leads on to the next point.

e) We are to assume personal responsibility for our lives

It is important that we never use any counselling technique which undermines someone's personal responsibility. There is an apparent contradiction in Galatians 6. In verse 2, we are told to carry one another's burdens, but in verse 5 it says each one should 'carry his own load'. In fact, the two words translated 'burden' and 'load' respectively are quite different in meaning. A 'burden' is a heavy load which we need help to carry, while the word for 'load' was used of a soldier's kitbag. No self-respecting soldier would expect someone else to carry his kit for him on a route march! So, while we are to help those burdened with troubles too hard for them to carry alone, we are not to undermine their personal responsibility for their own lives, as the context of verse 4 makes clear.

Indeed, the aim of all counselling is to help people accept responsibility for both their past actions and their reactions to hurt, rather than to take away their sense of personal responsibility. Otherwise there is a danger of people developing an unhealthy dependency on those who are counselling them. When I am counselling somebody, I always emphasise their own personal responsibility to 'walk free' of whatever problem, or even evil spirit, has affected them. Ezekiel 18:2 teaches us that we should not live according to the proverb of that day, 'The fathers eat sour grapes, and the children's teeth are set on edge'. Probably none of us have used those exact words recently! However, we may have said, 'Well, if you had had the father I had...', 'Well, with my upbringing...' or 'I was so hurt, you see, that it is not surprising that...' All these familiar expressions can be a way of avoiding our own personal responsibility.

f) Teaching is important

In Mark 6:34, it is recorded that Jesus had compassion on the crowds and responded to their lost and harassed condition ('like sheep without a shepherd') by 'teaching them many things'. Whatever their other needs, He responded first to their pressing need to receive truth because, as He Himself said on another occasion, 'If you hold to my teaching, you are really my disciples. Then you will know the truth, and the truth will set you free' (John 8:31–32). Whatever people's needs and hurts, we must avoid offering mere sympathy without teaching them truth. It is as we understand truth and apply it to our lives that we can walk free, particularly when that takes place in the context of a commitment to follow Jesus and live a life of discipleship.

3 A biblical view of mankind

This is very important because it is in our understanding of human nature that we differ from so many secular psychological theories.

a) Evaluation of some secular psychological theories

This section comments very briefly on some of the theories that are used to form the basis of some secular counselling. I recognise that in a short guide like this, it is not possible to do full justice to any of them. However, this section is included for two reasons:

● Some of these theories have influenced practices of counselling within the Christian church.

● Some of these theories form the basis of what many people outside the church believe about how we function as human beings, even though most may be totally unaware of what the underlying theories actually are. As we counsel and disciple new converts, for example, we may find that much of their thinking is based on popular psychotherapeutic ideas. A very helpful book which analyses the various theories underlying psychotherapeutic thought today is *Roots and Shoots* by Dr Roger Hurding.[1] (See note at end of chapter.)

i) Behaviourist theory

This theory gives much credence to cause and effect and to the ability to shape and control appropriate human behaviour in particular circumstances. Names such as Pavlov and Skinner are associated with this theory. Pavlov is well known for his experiments on dogs, in which he was able to condition their behaviour so that they salivated upon the ringing of a bell rather than when food was put before them. Many experiments have been carried out to show how animal behaviour can be influenced by the conditions in which they are placed. Skinner argued that all behaviour is essentially a product of conditioning, and referred to actions that we can take in order to reinforce positive behaviour. There is, of course, some truth in this. For example, we discipline our children in order to bring about behaviour change. However, the corollary – that human behaviour is entirely conditioned by environment – is not a biblical view. For example, improvements in environment such as modern housing developments replacing traditional slums have certainly not always produced a corresponding improvement in behaviour. Adam and Eve sinned when they were in a wonderful environment! Behaviourist theories do not do full justice to the complexity of human personality, including creativity, imagination and particularly faith in God, the consequences of which can neither be measured and scrutinised by scientific means, nor explained away in terms of the conditioning of behaviour.

ii) Freud

Much Freudian and Jungian theory again underlies the way many people think, even though in academic terms much of it is now discredited. Freud saw man as the victim of primitive subconscious urges, particularly sexual. This led to a popular way of thinking that pushing down and denying these urges – as it is alleged religion does – is unhealthy and a cause of neurosis. Many Freudian words such as 'subconscious', 'repression', 'Oedipus complex', 'Freudian slip' and 'regression' have become part of our vocabulary and, more significantly, part of our worldview – the way we think about ourselves and our environment. 'Let it all hang out' became a rallying cry in the

1960s when permissiveness was thought to lead to a healthier psychological lifestyle. The philosophy of 'If it feels good, do it' is a direct descendant of Freudian thought, and its results are now seen in a society with few absolute values concerning right and wrong behaviour, and increased rejection and alienation as a result of the break-up of family life. Freud was less simplistic than the popular adaptations of his theories, and did much to help us understand the complex nature of personality and the role of the subconscious, as we can understand similarly from Psalm 139:14: 'We are fearfully and wonderfully made.'

iii) Non-directive counselling

This view is very influential in counselling today. It originated with Carl Rogers and starts with the premise that human nature is basically good. People are therefore encouraged to talk about their situation, their feelings and the possible solutions, while the counsellor listens carefully and then reflects back to them what they are saying. The person is thus helped to a clearer understanding of their own situation and is able to make autonomous choices which, because human nature is viewed as basically good, will on the whole be helpful to them. This fits in with the more general view today that there are no absolutes and that 'what is right for you' may not be 'right for me'. The result is that people come into the Christian church wanting help, but unwilling to receive direction because they hold the attitude that 'nobody can tell me what to do' or 'my opinion is just as valid as yours'. While there is much that we can learn from this theory of counselling in terms of caring skills such as listening and reflecting back, we cannot accept its non-directive nature, which ignores the reality of sin, views human beings as self-governing and separates counselling from discipling. Surely the point is that as Christians, all our opinions should be submitted to the lordship of Christ and to truth as revealed in Scripture. Biblical Christian counselling cannot be non-directive because it must draw people's attention to the directions given by God in Scripture.

iv) Transactional analysis (TA)

This theory has been particularly influential on much Christian counselling, and there are things we can learn from it. It describes people as having an 'ego state', or system of feelings, which motivates a related set of behaviour patterns. These behaviour patterns can be reinforced by positive or negative 'strokes' – encouragements that help us onward, or discouragements that get in our way.

In the 'parent' state, we react towards other people by assuming an unconscious superiority to them which may either be prejudiced and critical or nurturing and patronising. In the 'child' state, we allow others to dominate us and react by either submitting and assuming a 'victim' mentality, or by rebelling. The objective is to attain the 'adult' state in which we are able to be autonomous, responsible for our own actions and able to make informed, reasoned decisions.

TA alternatively describes people as occupying various 'life positions'. 'I'm not OK, you're OK' means that I feel bad about myself but good about other people, and TA suggests that this can be changed by positive strokes. 'I'm not OK, you're not OK' is the position in which a person feels bad about themselves and the rest of the world. It is suggested that positive stroking cannot overcome this double rejection of self and others. 'I'm OK, you're not OK' is the attitude of 'I'll look after number one', without any regard for others. The objective is to reach the 'I'm OK, you're OK' position in which we accept ourselves and others for who we are. TA is somewhat pessimistic in saying that most people do not achieve this life position.

TA uses the term 'script' to describe the basic direction which governs people's lives as a result of what happened to them in their early years, and labels people as 'winners' or 'losers'. Some writers conclude that a person's 'script' is decided by the time they are six years old, and will not change unless that person is one of the few who are able to leave their 'script' behind through help from transactional analysis.

Clearly, there is much here that is helpful, but again, we do not accept TA's view of human autonomy, or its pessimistic lack of expectation that people can change. Praise God that redemption through the cross of Christ and the new life given to us in new birth can bring much greater hope than that! Furthermore, our objective is not to be 'OK', but first to recognise our unworthiness before God, as Peter did when he said to Jesus, 'Go away from me, Lord; I am a sinful man!' (Luke 5:8). From this 'life position' we can then experience the transforming nature of the work of Jesus and the Holy Spirit.

b) Mankind is the peak of God's creation, created in the image of God

This is described in Genesis 1–2. We need to note that both male and female are created in God's image. We need also to note that the emphasis is on man in fellowship and community, rather than on his own. The first thing that God said of Adam was that it was not good for man to be alone. Though in its immediate context this goes on to describe marriage, marriage is certainly not the only application of that scripture. We were created in the image of a God who is Trinity. This means a God who in His essence is community – one God, three persons. As those created in His image, we are therefore created for fellowship and community. It is sadly true that in such community we can become hurt and retreat behind individualistic defence mechanisms. However, our objective in setting people free is not just to make them feel better but to help them relate to the community of which they are called to be part.

Genesis 1–2 also describes mankind as endued with creativity and with choice and responsibility. Furthermore, the fact that we are all created in the image of God means we all have value. However, you will not find in this course an emphasis on 'self-esteem' or even 'self-worth'. I believe we all have value because we are created by God, and are made in His image, rather than because of any intrinsic, independent value we perceive ourselves to have.

c) Man is a unity

1 Thessalonians 5:23 refers to our whole spirit, soul and body. Some use this scripture to emphasise the division of man into different components. However, I believe the purpose of that scripture is rather to emphasise our unity! In other words, what happens in my emotions can affect me physically. What happens physically can affect my emotions. What happens to me spiritually can affect both my body and my emotions.

d) Mankind has fallen

Genesis 3 tells us about this. Notice the effect of the Fall upon Adam and Eve. There was guilty fear, acute self-consciousness, and a bias towards wrongdoing and arrogant independence. The rebellion expressed in the Fall has affected every part of human life in broken relationships:

- Broken relationship with God, so that apart from the work of Christ we are now spiritually dead.

- Broken relationships with others – family and community became affected by the Fall, with Adam blaming his wife (Genesis 3:12), Cain killing his brother Abel (Genesis 4:8), and society deteriorating to the point where, in Noah's day, corruption and violence were endemic and widespread (Genesis 6:5).

- Nature itself is affected (Romans 8:20–22).

- Sin does its work within ourselves so that we do not experience the peace of God (Romans 7:14–24).

When approaching Christian counselling, we need to recognise the fallen condition from which Christians have been saved. It is not, as modern-day humanists would have us believe, that we are inherently good, but rather that apart from God's grace and the new birth we have a bias towards evil. This also has a bearing on how far we can help those outside the church. Obviously part of our kingdom ministry is to bring God's comfort to those outside the church. However, we must always recognise that they can only be fully restored as they come to Christ and have the power of the cross dealing with the effects of the Fall in their lives.

e) Yet despite the Fall, the image of God is not completely destroyed and our derived intrinsic value therefore remains

This is demonstrated by the fact that the creating of man in God's image is referred to again after the flood in Genesis 9:5-6.

f) Mankind is restorable in Christ

According to 2 Corinthians 3:18, we are being transformed through a process of sanctification until the image of God is more clearly seen in us. Helping one another to be free of issues from our past, and giving biblical counsel, are part of this process. In our standing before God and in our reflecting of His image, there is no difference between male or female, between races or between classes and backgrounds (Galatians 3:28).

Our relationship with God has been restored through the cross. This means that our relationships with each other are being restored, as we are members of one body. We can also see a restoration within our own selves and can experience the peace of God which passes understanding. Eventually in the new heaven and new earth, everything will be restored and nature itself will be as God originally intended it to be. Until that time there will always be a process, a journey towards wholeness that remains to some extent incomplete. Sometimes we can make well-meaning promises to people about their achieving wholeness now. Actually, until we are in the new heaven and new earth, until we are with Christ, we will always be on a journey and not have arrived. There will be issues that arise throughout our lives which we need to learn to handle in a godly way. We must be careful not to make false promises to people, otherwise, when all is not 'sweetness and light', they may become disillusioned with the process of Christian sanctification.

Our value is re-emphasised in Christ. We all have value because we are created in God's image. In addition, for the Christian, it is also true that we have value through the grace of God as those who are now in Christ. We are accepted as Christ is accepted. We are loved as Christ is loved (John 17:23).

So we see again that we must be careful to guard against a clinical, professional/client attitude coming into Christian counselling in the church. Our attitude in all our relationships within the church should be that we consider the other better than ourselves (see Philippians 2:3). This applies in the counselling context, whatever background or problems the person being counselled may present.

4 Use of spiritual gifts in Christian counselling

We expect God to move in power as we pray with a person needing help. We expect to see this both in terms of evident inner effects that transform character and also through the gifts of the Holy Spirit as we meet in a team with the person. I believe that the moving of the Holy Spirit brings an 'economy' to our counselling, though this does not mean we ignore legitimate caring skills. When a team of two is meeting to pray for a Christian, we can expect the Holy Spirit to move and the presence of Jesus to be experienced as the 'three are gathered in his name' (Matthew 18:20). I have often found that not only do those on the team receive spiritual gifts which help the situation forward, but so does the person with whom we are praying, who must be seen not as a client needing our help but as a fellow member of the body of Christ, working together with those counselling, to see transformation in their life. God is able to give His gifts to each one present.

5 Particular gifts helpful in counselling

a) The gift of tongues

When we are praying and counselling, it can be helpful to pray in tongues quietly to build ourselves up. I have also found that the gift of tongues opens us up to the presence of God, which enables other gifts of the Holy Spirit to flow. Sometimes we can bring brief petitions to God in tongues when we are not sure what to do or say next. Just occasionally I have seen the gift of tongues used as a sign. I remember somebody coming for counsel high on drugs. I was about to give up on the session, as

I could get nowhere with the person in that condition, when I felt I should just pray over them in tongues. As I did, they became instantly stone-cold sober, and that very miracle opened them to receiving the counsel I was about to give.

b) Interpretation of tongues

The gift of the interpretation of tongues is the supernatural revelation through the Holy Spirit which enables us to communicate, in the language of the listener, not so much a word for word 'translation' as the gist or 'dynamic equivalent' of a tongue. I believe this can happen in a counselling time as well as in a public meeting. I remember one occasion when I was praying with somebody in a tongue and the person counselling with me immediately received an interpretation and expressed in prayer to God the longing of a child for the response of a father. At that moment the person being counselled burst into tears because that interpretation had expressed the inner longing of their heart because of a lack of relationship with their own father.

c) Prophecy

Prophecy is the ability given by God to receive from Him and then communicate to others an immediate message of God. It can come in words, in pictures or in actions. Often God gives a picture which hits the mark as far as the person being counselled is concerned, even if it means little to the person who receives it. Pictures or prophetic actions, provided they are initiated by the Spirit of God, can help a person to freedom. However, we must be very careful that we do not turn what is prophetic into a methodology. God may give pictures or dramatic actions to help a particular person in a particular situation – this is, after all, the essence of the prophetic – but this must not then be allowed to become a fixed method which we always employ when helping people with a similar problem.

d) Discernment of spirits

This is the supernatural gift of perception given by God to enable us to distinguish the motivating spirit behind certain words or deeds. The origin can be human (for example, someone may be communicating out of their own hurt or frustration something which would appear to be very spiritual), divine (of God) or demonic (from the enemy). The gift of discernment of spirits is essential when we are ministering to people who may be demonised (see Seminar 6).

e) Words of wisdom

This is the special ability that God gives us to receive insight from Him about how a particular situation is to be resolved. This is very important when we are counselling. We must not rely just on our own experience or understanding but must be open to God to be able to say wise words which unlock situations and minister freedom.

f) Word of knowledge

This is a supernatural revelation of facts about a person or situation which are not learned through the efforts of the natural mind but are fragments of knowledge, freely given by God, disclosing the truth which the Holy Spirit wishes to be made known concerning a particular person or situation. A word of knowledge does not always give the full story about somebody's problem. It may, however, give a 'fragment of knowledge' which unlocks the situation. It can be received in many ways. Sometimes it is simply a flood of thought or strong impression. It can also come in dreams, visions, pictures, or relevant Scripture verses which we did not know were relevant until we had spoken them out.

g) Gift of faith

This is the supernatural surge of confidence from the Holy Spirit whereby we receive a certainty and assurance that God is about to act. This is obviously very helpful when praying for people's physical healing but we could also expect to experience it when we are praying for people to be set free from the effects of hurts or trauma upon their lives.

h) Miracles and gifts of healing

We believe that God will intervene in these supernatural ways.

6 How do we move more in these gifts?

a) It is important that when we are counselling others we are genuinely open to the Holy Spirit and have our own minds less full of all our own ideas, doubts, frustrations with apparent lack of breakthrough, tensions from our own lives, etc. We need to learn how to put these things behind us when we come to minister to others. It is good to pray 'Come, Holy Spirit' not as a formula but as a deep desire to experience the manifest presence of God. I believe the Holy Spirit dynamic is essential in Christian counselling

b) Through worship and prayer. As we worship God and seek Him for spiritual gifts, we have the firm promise of Scripture that He is ready to give them to us (Matthew 7:11; Luke 11:13).

c) We do need to learn how to move more in the gifts of the Spirit. This does involve taking risks, but if we are in a team environment what we say can be tested by the others present. It is important also that we learn to minister first with somebody more experienced than ourselves, not just because of their counselling skill but also because of their greater understanding of how the gifts of the Holy Spirit work.

[1] Roger Hurding, *Roots and Shoots*, Hodder & Stoughton 1986.

Essential Foundations of Salvation and Baptism in the Holy Spirit

1 Introduction

Having given a biblical framework for the ministry of counselling and caring in Seminar 1, we now come to deal with the first practical issues of how to help those who come to us in need of being healed and set free.

We have already noted that while it is part of our kingdom ministry to bring God's comfort to those outside the church, people can be fully restored only as they come to Christ and have the power of the cross dealing with the effects of sin in their lives. We therefore need to be ready to lead enquirers to Christ and see that godly foundations of faith, repentance, baptism in water and baptism in the Holy Spirit are established in their lives as essential first steps towards freedom.

It is not only non-Christians who may lack these foundations. I have often noticed, when counselling Christians, that many of their problems are due to the fact that when they came to Christ, they did not clearly understand the process of salvation, either what was required of them or what God had done for them. In such circumstances, advice or prayer ministry which avoids addressing these foundational issues can at best fail to meet their real needs, and at worst can be counter-productive. People may be asking for help facing a particular issue, when their real need is to understand what repentance and the consequential renewing of the mind really involve.

Consequently, I make no apology for including a whole seminar on the essentials of salvation and baptism in the Holy Spirit in a guide on Christian counselling! In addition, since this guide is also intended to help Christians minister to people after church services or in other such contexts, it may well be that the person requesting help has actually come forward for salvation, or to be filled with the Holy Spirit. So counsellors or ministry teams must be well prepared to help people with these basics.

Before we consider the following four foundations in more detail, let us ensure that we have a clear understanding of the gospel ourselves, so that we can explain it simply and accurately to those seeking our help, in order to lead them to salvation. We need to be ready with a brief summary such as the following:

Jesus was born into the world as a man, lived a perfect life, died on a cross to carry the guilt of all our wrongdoing, rose again from death and now lives for ever. We need to repent of our wrong, believe in the truth about what God did on the cross and follow Jesus as our Lord, willing to obey Him in everything. We need to be baptised in water and receive the power of His Spirit to live a new life. We shall be saved from eternal punishment and be given eternal life.

2 Foundation of faith

Faith is very likely to be present with the Christian seeking help, but not necessarily with the non-Christian enquirer.

a) At its simplest, faith is the belief that God exists and responds to those who seek Him (Hebrews 11:6). It is the belief that Jesus died on the cross to save sinners and rose again from the dead (Romans 10:9).

b) Faith is a matter not only of believing facts, but of believing in a person. It involves the heart, not just the head (Romans 10:10), and is an attitude of trust and commitment, rather than merely the giving of intellectual assent. It implies acceptance of the lordship of Christ. We see the difference between 'head' faith and 'heart' faith in the story of the rich young ruler, who believed in God and lived by God's laws, but found himself unwilling to submit to Jesus' lordship by obeying His command to sell all he had and follow Jesus (Mark 10:17–22).

c) Faith is verbal (Romans 10:9). There is a powerful spiritual dynamic in speaking out in faith. Encourage people to pray their own prayer of accepting Christ, and to tell others what God has done for them.

d) Faith will result in works. Obedience to God's commands is the practical outworking of faith and the evidence that faith is genuine. We read in Acts 6:7 that 'a large number ... became obedient to the faith'. Be careful about announcing publicly that a person has 'become a Christian' before you have seen their 'works of faith' (James 2:14–26).

When Christians seek counsel for problems they face in their lives, it is important to ascertain whether they are really building their life on the foundation of faith. Are they secure in who they are in Christ, believing they are forgiven, unconditionally accepted and loved? Do they trust God for their past, present and future? This foundation is essential if Christians are to be effectively helped forward in overcoming the problems of life.

3 Foundation of repentance

The importance of repentance has often been underplayed and has sometimes resulted in Christians being troubled by sins from their past, long after their conversion.

a) Repentance should be specific. Matthew 1:21 tells us that Jesus came to save us from our 'sins', i.e. not just from 'sin' in general, but from our own particular sins. Therefore, when someone comes to Christ, we should expect them to repent of specific sins they have committed, not merely to express regret about general, vague, unidentified wrongdoing.

b) Repentance involves accepting responsibility for one's own sin, and not passing the buck by making excuses or blaming other people or circumstances for our own wrong behaviour. The following are examples of failure to take responsibility:

> 'It's not my fault – it's the way I was brought up. I didn't have a father, you see.'

'Anyone as depressed as I was...'

'I had been hurt so much...'

c) Repentance involves renunciation of sin; that is, a clear turning away from it, with a determination not to return to it. The Oxford Dictionary defines 'renounce' as 'abandon, surrender, give up, decline association with, withdraw from, discontinue'. All of these are helpful ways of understanding the necessity of radically separating ourselves from past sin.

d) Repentance should be audible. Spoken renunciation of sin is particularly important when sins have been habitual, obsessional or occultic. As has already been mentioned, there is a spiritual dynamic to speaking things out loud.

e) Repentance should be visible. When John the Baptist doubted the genuineness of his hearers' repentance, he challenged them to 'produce fruit in keeping with repentance' (Luke 3:8). Such 'fruit' may include:

- apologising and working to restore damaged relationships;
- restitution of stolen goods;
- getting rid of objects that lead to temptation or provide reminders and links with the person's past life. In Acts 19:19, for example, Ephesian Christian converts burnt their occultist literature.

f) There is a significant difference between repentance and regret. Regret may mean no more than a vague sadness or unease with one's past actions, expressed in such terms as 'It's a pity...' or 'If only...'. Repentance goes beyond regret and

- agrees with God's assessment of the action as sin;
- turns to God as the only and necessary source of forgiveness;
- turns from the sin and determines to do differently in future.

4 Foundation of baptism in water

In the New Testament, baptism in water was obviously explained as part of the gospel (Acts 2:38; 8:36), and is linked with starting the Christian life (Acts 2:41; 10:47; 22:14–16) and making disciples (Matthew 28:19–20).

Baptism involves a grave, which signifies the end of the old life and the beginning of the new. We die to sin in coming to Christ (Romans 6:5), and our baptism is our burial (Romans 6:3–4). This truth is very important in helping people to understand their freedom from sin in Christ.

A person should be baptised as soon as they have come to Christ and shown proof that they have repented (Acts 26:20). This could be as soon as the same day (Acts 10:48) or the same night (Acts 16:33).

If someone has not been baptised:

- they have missed the benefits of baptism;
- they have not been obedient to God's commands;
- they have missed out on what is biblically the first step in Christian discipleship.

5 Foundation of baptism in the Holy Spirit

a) What is baptism in the Holy Spirit?

i) It is the experience available to every Christian of receiving the power of the Holy Spirit and thus being enabled to use spiritual gifts, experience the assurance of God's love, and be effective in witnessing to Jesus and serving Him in the body of Christ, the church.

ii) It is a dynamic filling of the Holy Spirit. The word 'baptise' in Greek meant 'drench, soak, sink, overwhelm'. A person could be 'baptised' with sorrow or debt; a ship could be 'baptised' by waves coming over the side in a storm. So to be 'baptised' in the Holy Spirit suggests a powerful, possibly overwhelming experience of being filled with the power

and presence of God. Other words used in the New
Testament to describe this coming of Holy Spirit include:

- pour out (Acts 10:45)
- anoint (Acts 10:38)
- drink (John 7:37)
- come upon (Acts 1:8)
- fill (Ephesians 5:18)

iii) It is not the same as 'being touched' by the Holy Spirit
(falling or shaking), which can happen to unbelievers as
well as believers, e.g. to the soldiers who came to arrest
Jesus (John 18:6). Such an experience is a touch of God's
power, but is not baptism in the Holy Spirit. It can,
however, happen to those who have already been baptised
in the Spirit, causing them to know God's power even more.

iv) Baptism in the Holy Spirit is separate from conversion; it
may happen at about the same time, or at some subsequent
time. For example:

- The original disciples, the first to be filled with the Holy
  Spirit on the day of Pentecost (Acts 2:4), were already
  born again.
- In Caesarea, Cornelius's household received the Holy
  Spirit while Peter was still explaining the message of
  salvation to them (Acts 10:44)!
- In Ephesus, Paul found a group of believers who had not
  heard of the Holy Spirit, but were filled after his
  corrective ministry and teaching.

v) When a person is baptised in the Holy Spirit, it is clear to
them that it has happened (Galatians 3:2), and there is
usually audible evidence that makes it clear to others:

- speaking in tongues is mentioned several times in Acts,
  when details are given of people receiving the Holy
  Spirit (Acts 2:4; 10:46; 19:6);
- prophecy (Acts 19:6);
- an overflow of praise (Acts 10:46; Romans 8:15);
- boldness in witness (Acts 1:8).

b) The importance of baptism in the Spirit

i) Jesus taught His apostles about the importance of their being baptised in the Holy Spirit, as He reminded them after His resurrection, commanding them to wait in Jerusalem, until 'in a few days you will be baptised in the Holy Spirit' (Acts 1:4–5).

ii) On the day of Pentecost, Peter made it clear that the same experience of the Holy Spirit was available to all believers (Acts 2:17–18, 39).

iii) When Samaritan converts did not receive the Holy Spirit under Philip's ministry, the apostles Peter and John were sent to Samaria to rectify the situation (Acts 8:14–17).

iv) Paul, as we have already seen, quickly noticed a missing dimension in the Ephesian believers' lives and asked them, 'Did you receive the Holy Spirit when you believed?' On hearing their ignorance of the whole subject, Paul checked their spiritual credentials carefully, and finally laid hands on them so that 'the Holy Spirit came on them and they spoke in tongues and prophesied' (Acts 19:1–6).

v) Christians often seek help with problems when they have not experienced this fresh power necessary for living the Christian life. Biblical counsel will no doubt be helpful, but without the foundational experience of baptism in the Holy Spirit, people are being robbed of the power God has made available to them for overcoming the issues they may be facing. They also need to be encouraged to go on being filled continually with the Holy Spirit (Ephesians 5:18) and not regard their baptism in the Holy Spirit as a one-off event which recedes into the past and loses its freshness and effectiveness over time.

c) How to pray for people to be baptised in the Holy Spirit

i) The person should be sure in their own mind that this is a biblical experience. If necessary, explain it to them from relevant Bible verses such as some of those mentioned in this chapter. Faith comes by knowledge of the truth.

ii) Encourage people into a position of faith, so that they expect to receive the Holy Spirit when they are prayed for. Do not impose prayer on them if they are passive or unbelieving – this will tend to be unfruitful. Ask questions such as 'Are you ready to drink now?' Explain that they need to 'drink' – it is not something imposed on them or 'done to them' without their co-operation.

iii) Reservations and obstacles may need clearing up before you pray. Watch for these as you look to see if faith is dawning.

- Unrepented sin may need to be confessed and brought to God for forgiveness.

- Some people hold back with reservations such as 'Am I worthy?' or 'Am I ready?' or 'Is this the time yet?' We need to point out to them that after the day of Pentecost, nobody was told to 'wait for the Holy Spirit'. Furthermore, baptism in the Spirit is not to do with Christian maturity; it is available to the newest of Christians. It is often helpful to share testimonies of people who have been baptised in the Spirit – perhaps your own testimony or that of someone you have prayed for.

iv) Explain that you will lay hands on them (Acts 8:18; 19:6). Then lay hands on the person and pray for them. It is also good to encourage them to express their thirst and ask for themselves, because this kindles faith.

v) Expect them to experience some of the gifts of the Spirit. You may need to explain that if the person is to speak in tongues, they have to open their mouth and use their vocal cords and speak. Acts 2:4 tells us that the believers began to speak as the Holy Spirit gave them the words; God does not turn us into puppets and move our mouths for us! When people begin to speak in tongues, they often feel foolish and think they are 'making it up'. Reassure them that this is a gift from God (Luke 11:11–13; 1 Corinthians 14:2).

vi) Do not say 'Now you have received' when there is no evidence that they have. It is true that the manifestation of spiritual gifts such as speaking in tongues may come a little while afterwards, but the person should have the witness of the Holy Spirit within them that they have received, and be expecting to exercise gifts.

vii) If nothing happens:

- Re-check the steps above.
- Sometimes, people just need to 'loosen up' a bit. David Pawson suggests sending people away by themselves to jump and dance and sing and shout until they get over their inhibitions and do not mind who sees them.[1]
- Sometimes there is a delay. Encourage people to keep asking and keep trusting that God will meet with them. I have known people who have been prayed for to receive the baptism with the Holy Spirit and nothing seems to 'happen' at the time. However, subsequently and often unexpectedly, God meets them and floods them with His power and love. My own wife experienced this. Nothing seemed to happen when she was prayed for and then suddenly the Holy Spirit came upon her when she was hoovering the carpets in our house!
- Sometimes people need ministry to areas of rejection and self-rejection before they can receive.

6 Conclusion

It is an important part of genuine biblical counselling to ensure that these foundations of faith, repentance and baptism in water and in the Holy Spirit are in place in the lives of those we seek to help. Our objective is to see people set free and able to overcome difficulties. We are not serving them thoroughly if we fail to help them establish these essential foundations for effective Christian life, freedom and fruitfulness. The later chapters in this guide will equip you to go on from here in helping to set people free. In our enthusiasm to develop further biblically based methodologies, please let us not rush on too hastily from a careful consideration of these basics.

[1] David Pawson, *The Normal Christian Birth*, Hodder & Stoughton 1989.

Caring Skills

1 The importance of listening

a) As Christian carers we must learn to listen on two levels:
- to what the person being counselled is saying;
- to the Holy Spirit.

Having the physical capacity to hear is not necessarily the same as listening carefully and with understanding, as Jesus pointed out when He said, 'He who has ears, let him hear' (Matthew 13:9). We can seem to hear, yet fail to listen properly to one another or to God

- when we are more concerned with thinking about what we want to say than with what the other person is trying to tell us;
- when we are absorbed in a mêlée of activity that distracts our attention. (Pastors can sometimes be like this after a Sunday service, so it may be better to suggest meeting up on another occasion, rather than fail to give full attention!)

It is important to cultivate an inner openness and receptiveness that allows us to truly listen, without imposing our own agenda or preconceptions.

b) Do not be too quick to advise. We should be less preoccupied with giving answers and helpful comments than with listening and hearing what the person is saying. It is probably difficult for them to bare their heart and speak about their inner pain, and our ability to listen sensitively and attentively is very important to them. Even when we believe God has revealed to us the answer to their problem, we need to be cautious. Words of knowledge do not need to be blurted out immediately. Many people need to express their feelings and experiences first, before they are ready to hear us suggest the true source of their difficulties. Sometimes our relationship with the person will be such that we can come out quickly with what we believe God has said, but generally we must listen first and not be too quick to speak (James 1:19).

c) Good listening involves being more aware of the other person than of yourself. Rather than being concerned with your own 'ministry of counselling', focus on the person who needs help. Do not focus on thinking about what you are going to say when the person has finished. If you have a lot of experience of helping people in this way, do not concentrate on the answers you know from past experience. The person should be able to feel that they are very important to you, not that they are one item on your production line.

d) Focus on the feelings that lie buried beneath the words. The real issue is often not the factual account of what has happened to someone, but the emotions that lie beneath the words, i.e. the way they feel about what has happened.

e) Reflect back to the person the content and emotions contained in what they have said. Many people are not good at telling a coherent story, and it may take time for you to understand it well enough to reflect back to them both the content and emotions of what they have told you. It is important to do this, in order to be sure that you and the other person both know you have heard and understood them correctly.

f) Be non-judgemental. Do not express your horror! Reactions like 'Surely you didn't do that!' or 'I didn't know people did things like that!' will not inspire confidence that you are the right person for them to come to with their problem. This does not mean that you will not offer them correction at the appropriate time.

2 Recognising defence mechanisms

Most of us have learned to cover up what is really going on in our minds and hearts. We impose various layers, like fig leaves, over our true condition. These methods of concealment are known as 'defence mechanisms'. They are the varied ways in which the human personality tends to act, in order to defend itself against exposure and rejection. It is important that we understand something of these defence mechanisms so that we can help people to face the real issues in their lives and thus make progress as disciples of Jesus. Selwyn Hughes has an excellent chapter on this subject in his book *How to Help a Friend*,[1] and I am indebted to him for much of the material in this section. The most common defence mechanisms are as follows.

a) Compensation can be described as leaning backwards to avoid falling forwards. It is the covering up or disguising of an undesirable trait by developing a desirable one, usually of a contrasting nature. For example, someone may make themselves very busy in Christian service in order to cover up their insecurity with a sense of 'usefulness'. Someone may compensate for fearfulness by acting as if they are not afraid, 'whistling in the dark'. Sublimation is very similar to compensation; it is the transforming of inner conflicts into socially accepted and useful goals.

b) Displacement is taking out one's negative emotions on the wrong person. For example, a husband who has had a trying day at work may overreact to a small incident at home by letting out all the anger and frustration that has built up during the day, leaving his wife wondering what she has done to provoke such an outburst. When someone has been badly hurt, there may be a lot of hidden anger which is then 'dumped' onto someone else who is not responsible for engendering it, and may in fact be the very person who is trying to help them! They are not rejecting the help, though it may feel like that to the counsellor, but simply letting out stored-up anger and expressing it towards the wrong person. Pastors and others in authority in a local church may have anger expressed towards them, which is not really personal (though it may feel like it!) but represents anger against authority figures, which has been there for years.

c) Projection is blaming others. For example, when Adam was caught sinning, he blamed Eve ('the woman you put here with me', Genesis 3:12). Or again, someone who gives in to bad temper may blame other people for annoying them. Displacement and projection can run together. Where somebody has been badly hurt, they may begin to blame those currently in authority over them, such as a counsellor or church leader. Learn to endure this and do not take it personally!

d) Introjection is picking up other people's mannerisms because one feels insecure about oneself. This shows itself, for example, in someone who behaves differently when in different company, or who imitates the speech, mannerisms or attitudes of people he admires.

e) Rationalisation is giving a fictional but apparently valid reason to justify behaviour now exposed as wrong or inappropriate that was really based on other motives.

f) Denial can be a refusal to admit to sin, or to pain that has been suffered. It is a way of avoiding confronting experiences and memories that are too painful to face up to, and is often a difficult thing to break through until the Holy Spirit begins to work in people's lives.

g) Fantasy is the misuse of the imagination, and often goes hand in hand with denial. A person may deny the reality of painful things in their lives and memories, and instead invent an alternative reality which is less difficult to deal with. This may consist of imagining something else is happening (other than what actually is happening), or of imagining wonderful things at will (creating a private fantasy world).

h) Regression is the tendency to revert to an earlier behaviour or form of expression, e.g. thumb-sucking, rocking, speaking in a 'little girl' voice. It is an attempt to invoke other people's pity by appearing helpless, like a little child, and thus avoid having to take responsibility for one's life and behaviour.

i) Idealisation is living one's life through other people who appear more successful, and putting them on a pedestal. For example, parents who were not well educated may idealise their child who has gone to university, and live through them (which can, incidentally, be very hard on the child!). It is very painful for the people who put someone on a pedestal, when their 'idol' inevitably falls from grace and disappoints them.

j) Reaction formation is the common tendency to be extremely critical of faults in other people which are, in fact, the faults we dislike in ourselves. A common example is that someone who gossips may dislike themselves for doing so, but will come down very hard on others who gossip rather than deal with the fault in themselves.

k) Deflection is evading certain ideas or thoughts by deflecting the thought processes around the painful ideas or avoiding talking about them by changing the subject and moving on to something else.

l) 'Conversion' is the transformation of inner mental or psychological conflict into a physical manifestation. (NB This is not biblical conversion!)

m) Withdrawal is a reaction of extreme shyness in which a person will avoid contact with others, perhaps by sitting alone or not speaking unless approached.

n) Isolation is similar to fantasy, and is an extreme defence mechanism in which one's thoughts are divorced from one's emotions. The results include an inability to make relationships, and a tendency to develop obsessions and compulsive behaviour.

3 Balancing counselling and prayer ministry

There are two dangers to be aware of as we consider the subject of counselling and praying for people.

- On the one hand, we may counsel, listen and advise extensively, without ever coming to the point of inviting the Holy Spirit in to do what we cannot do.

- On the other hand, we may be too quick to start praying, when we actually need to listen to the person (and to God) to find out what the problem is, and talk to them about how they need to live differently in order for healing to be effective.

4 The power of words

Words are very, very powerful! When God spoke, He created a world. The 'positive and negative strokes' referred to in transactional analysis are often in the form of words. Negative words said over us can act very powerfully to our detriment. For example, 'You've never been any good at that' or 'You're always starting things, but you never finish anything' may be historically true but, when spoken in that way, can act with binding power. They become curses over us and act like self-fulfilling prophecies. We need to break the power of such words over people. And we need to take care that we use words positively and constructively with those we are endeavouring to help.

a) Speak words of encouragement, not discouragement. James talks about how powerful the tongue is (James 3:1–12). We should consider how people feel when we have spoken to them. Do our words build them up or pull them down?

b) Avoid responding to people with trite and insensitive phrases such as:
   - 'You need to have more faith, don't you?'
   - 'Praise the Lord anyway!'
   - 'We all have days like that.'
   - 'That happens to us all.'

These may be true, but are inappropriate at that point. They are not likely to help and encourage the person who may have found it very difficult to summon up enough courage to come to us with their problem!

c) Avoid responding by immediately recounting a story of how you were once in a similar situation. Sometimes it can be helpful to tell of our own experience, but not until we have shown we understand theirs. They are not concerned with our experience, but with their own, and we need to meet them where they are and listen in order to bring them through.

d) Avoid coming up immediately with a solution, as this can make the person feel inadequate when they have struggled and failed to solve the problem themselves. Furthermore, in the end our objective is for them with God's help to take responsibility for their own lives, not just to follow our advice without thinking about it.

e) Use words of knowledge sensitively to spark off a line of enquiry, rather than bringing the word of knowledge directly. Jesus, for example, said to the Samaritan woman at the well, 'Go, call your husband' (John 4:16). He knew that she had no husband, but used that word of knowledge in an open-ended way which left her free to respond or not, rather than bringing a direct statement that gave her no choice.

f) Avoid acting on words of knowledge without confirmatory remembered evidence. We must be very careful in our counselling not to lead people into 'recalling' false memories. Our memories do play tricks, and there have been cases of secular counsellors inducing false memories of abuse based on misreading certain symptoms. In the context of Christian care and counselling, we must be very careful not to misuse words of knowledge or apparent symptoms in the same way. It is very important that such conclusions are confirmed from the person's own memory without inappropriate suggestions. Be particularly careful in this context when dealing with abuse and demonic activity in past generations.

5 Understanding body language

Secular studies of this subject have suggested that there are three aspects to our communication with other people, and have estimated that our words carry only 7% of our message, while our tone of voice carries 38% and our non-verbal body language 55%.

I personally would add that the condition of our own spirit also communicates. If we are anxious or angry, or are trying to push our own solution at the person, that will be communicated to them non-verbally, as will, on the other hand, our genuine concern and love. In other words, it is not just what we say that gets our message across, but how we say it. This raises two questions:

● As we listen, do we give the impression that we are really focused on the person who is speaking to us, or that we would rather be giving our attention to someone else, or be watching football on the television?

● And what about the person we are caring for: what can their body language tell us about their condition and how to help them?

a) Cultivating good body language

i) Focus directly on the person with whom you are talking. Don't look past them, or out of the window! On the other hand, avoid leaning forward in a confrontational stance that makes the person feel threatened.

ii) Don't get too close, but respect people's 'personal space'. Some need more personal space than others, and if you get too close, they will edge away from you. Avoid unnecessary physical contact, even when you come to pray with them. If you intend to lay hands on them, tell them what you are going to do and respect their wishes if they do not want to be touched. Don't 'crowd' people, e.g. don't push your face against theirs.

iii) Use eye contact. Look them directly in the eye; don't look past them or over them, or at the colour of their shoes or the pattern on their sweater.

iv) Match your facial expression to what the person is telling you. Don't sit grinning when someone is telling you something distressing! This can, of course, be taken too far. There is no need to imitate every change of expression in the person talking to you, or to weep copiously at every sad story.

b) Observe the body language of the person you are caring for

Body language can express a range of unspoken attitudes and reactions including:

- cutting off from the immediate situation because they find it threatening;

- insecurity about your acceptance of them or ability to help them;

- fear of what might be going to happen;

- closing off because of unwillingness to express emotions.

c) Encourage an open body attitude in the person you are praying with

It is hard for someone to be inwardly open to receiving from God if their outward body posture is closed and defensive. Encourage people to be relaxed, to sit or stand comfortably, to raise their head and open their hands, palms upwards, as if ready to receive – not that God is depending on this of course; He can break through anyway!

d) The other 'body language' – effects of 'spiritual' activity

When the Holy Spirit comes upon us, our bodies cannot always take what God is doing and therefore may react in various ways. We have to be cautious about labelling certain body reactions as definitely denoting particular things the Holy Spirit is doing. Often it is only afterwards that we find out for sure what was happening.

i) Falling

● Falling can be an indication of the peace of God or the power of God coming on someone.

● It can be a sort of 'spiritual anaesthetic' which relaxes the person when God wants to minister to their emotions.

● It can be a closing off, when the person themselves shuts off from what God is doing, as if to say, 'That's enough'.

● It can be an indication of demonisation. Demons fell down before the presence of Jesus (Mark 3:11).

● It can happen to non-Christians as well as Christians, so don't assume everything necessary has happened just because the person has fallen. Continue to pray for someone who has fallen, until you are satisfied in your spirit that this is no longer necessary.

ii) Shaking

● Shaking can be evidence of the power of God at work.

● It may indicate that healing is taking place, or the releasing of emotions.

● It may be a reaction of anger.

● It may indicate demonisation.

iii) Screaming

● Screaming can indicate that deep hurts are being released.

● It can indicate demonisation. The gift of discernment of spirits may help us to distinguish, but it is helpful to apply other tests as well and certainly not assume that it is demonic. Seminar 6 will help you concerning the discernment of the demonic. I would tend to assume that such problems are emotional unless I find on further investigation that there is evidence of demonic presence. In any case, I would not encourage such screaming to go on without helping the person to stop and talk over what the problem is.

iv) Weeping
- Weeping can indicate emotional release, or the healing of emotions.

v) Laughter
- Laughter can be a release of joy, or a release of a 'burden'. It is carefree but not careless.

- It can also be a 'laugh of faith', like Sarah's (Genesis 21:6; contrast Genesis 18:12). When a word comes to us saying that God will use us in a certain way, or do a certain thing in us, the initial reaction may be a laugh of unbelief, which then, like Sarah's, becomes a laugh of faith that 'God will use me'.

vi) Other possible physical effects
The following can be indications that the Holy Spirit is moving, or at least that there is spiritual activity:

- 'drunkenness' (Acts 2:15; Ephesians 5:18)
- twitching, parts of the body moving
- eyelids fluttering abnormally
- hot spots (a sudden concentration of heat in a part of someone's body and an indication of where to focus prayer, if appropriate)
- heat
- hands quivering, tingling

However, there are not always such effects. We must seek God, not particular dramatic effects, and the important thing is fruit in changed lives. Though the above is given for guidance, we must not imagine we can systematise God or work it all out. He and the effects of His Spirit remain beyond us.

It is important for people to find out what was going on when unusual things were happening to them, so that they know what God has done, and do not just have a 'wacky' experience to look back on or to seek in the future for its own sake.

6 Empathy

Empathy literally means 'feeling into' someone else's situation and problem as if we were experiencing it ourselves. It is identifying sufficiently with the person to feel their anguish or despair. Some people have a natural ability to empathise.

a) We need to be aware, on a moment-to-moment basis, of the feelings of the person we are counselling, as they share things with us. Their emotions may change from pain to anger and back again, and we need to develop sensitivity to this.

b) Sometimes empathy is a supernatural, God-given ability in a particular situation, enabling us to enter into another's pain and feel it as if it were our own. This can act as a spur to intercession, when we feel for the person and pray on their behalf, even if they are 'closed off' and not able to face the reality of their situation. We may feel pain and other emotions, which the person is unable to feel for themselves, almost like a word of knowledge, or gift of discernment of spirits. This may, indeed, be what God is doing to show us what the situation is, in order to help the person themselves realise what their true situation is.

7 Bringing correction

a) We need to challenge sin in the lives of those we are helping. If sin in a situation is left unrepented and unresolved, it becomes a blockage to healing and deliverance, and prevents the person from making proper progress generally.

b) Sin can cause people to 'lose' their healing. When Jesus healed the man at the pool of Bethesda (John 5:1–15), He warned him, 'Stop sinning or something worse may happen to you.' It is hard to imagine what could be worse than the 38 years of incapacitating illness the man had just been set free from, and Jesus' words are a serious warning of the debilitating effects sin can have, in terms of undermining our healing and spiritual walk.

c) Sin can also open a way for demons to come back after they have been expelled (Luke 11:24–26).

d) We need to confront sin when praying with people. It may be appropriate to say to them, 'I'm willing to pray for you that the root causes of your problem be dealt with, if you are willing to let go of your sin.' When people have been badly hurt, their pain can become an excuse to continue in sin, not necessarily in wrong actions, but more commonly in wrong attitudes and motives such as bitterness. We can minister God's healing power to the awful things that have happened to them, but they need to take responsibility for their reaction to those awful things.

e) We must maintain a balance between compassion and empathy on the one hand, and on the other hand, the recognition that unless people deal with their own sinful reactions and give and receive forgiveness, their healing will not come, or will not last. We are not being kind to approve a Christian continuing in sin, even though we are to accept them as a person.

8 Confidentiality

a) Confidentiality is absolutely essential. People can be hurt by gossip as much as by some of their original needs. Avoid saying such things as 'I'm just sharing this for prayer' or 'Don't tell anyone else but...'. If you ask somebody who has been counselling how they got on, unless you have been involved in prayer backing with the person's prior knowledge don't be offended if you are fobbed off with an 'OK'. There is no need for you to know anything confidential about another person's situation. Similarly, if you are the carer, don't be provoked by someone's well-meant enquiry into revealing confidential details about the person to whom you have been ministering.

b) 'Confidentiality' can be used as a weapon of manipulation, however. This can end up putting the counsellor in the difficult position of not being able to do anything about a problem. Someone may tell you something 'in confidence' that needs action to be taken, involving other people. People sinning in the issue may need to be spoken to. For example, a wife whose husband is beating her up may say, 'Don't tell my husband.' This manipulates us into the position of being able to do nothing about a situation that needs action. So confidentiality may not be absolute.

c) Within the context of a local church a better notion for counselling than confidentiality is 'stewardship of counsel'. This may be summarised as: 'I will not share your confidences with anybody who is not part of the problem or part of the solution.' This must be explained to people before we start to help them. For example, the person who has done the hurting may have to be spoken to. Those doing the counselling and prayer must be free to speak to those overseeing them who may, in turn, speak to the church elders in order to help bring about the solution. This is different from the confidentiality observed in many secular counselling organisations, because we are counselling in the context of discipleship and 'one-anothering' in the local church.

d) Total confidentiality is not always a safe or legal option. 'Please don't share this with the elders, as you are the only person I trust' may be flattering but may leave you exposed. There are situations where outside authorities, such as social services, must be informed, for example in cases of recent or continuing child abuse.

9 Avoid cross-sex counselling

By cross-sex counselling, I simply mean a man counselling a woman or a woman counselling a man. In secular counselling, where the relationship is that of professional and client, cross-sex counselling is considered normal and acceptable. A fundamental value in Christian counselling, however, is that we do not counsel or become involved in prayer ministry unless someone is present of the same sex as the person being counselled.

a) It can be helpful to have a man and a woman ministering together, whether it is a woman or a man being ministered to, because they can helpfully bring different perspectives to a situation. But we should not minister to a man unless another man is present, or to a woman unless another woman is present.

b) A man and a woman should not form a regular team together for counselling and prayer ministry, unless they are a married couple. It is better to choose the members of a team for a limited period or a one-off counselling situation, and check that the same pair are not put together in the next such team.

[1] Selwyn Hughes, *How to Help a Friend*, Kingsway 1981.

Physical Healing

1 Introduction

We believe that God is a God who heals, but we need to remember that God heals in different ways. It is important therefore that we do not find ourselves in bondage to the following:

a) Any particular method of healing. It is true that some who are powerfully anointed in healing ministry may themselves have faith for particular ways of operating. We must be careful that we do not seek to copy their methods without operating in the same faith or anointing.

b) Whether healing is instantaneous or a process over time. This has been quite an issue in recent church history. I recall at one time wondering whether it was a valid expression of faith to pray for somebody's healing a second time. There are some even today who say once we have prayed we must simply stand on the confession of our healing. John Wimber helped many of us to see that sometimes healing can be a process. We can pray several times and also, as we will see later, need on occasions to get to the roots of a particular sickness in order to see the person healed and stay healed. Though this understanding is very helpful, it can have the unintended effect of reducing faith for instantaneous healing. We can fall into the trap of developing a new method where we always have to find out what the roots of an illness are instead of simply stepping out in faith. We need to hold these in tension.

2 Growing faith

It is true that in the Western world we do have a battle for faith in relation to physical healing. I believe that many of us are finding that we are now seeing more healing than we used to, praise God. However, we are battling against the stronghold of the Western worldview. This means that we tend to believe only what we can see or explain rationally, and therefore regard what is physical as more 'real' than what is spiritual. So we may find that because we have explained sickness through our analysis of viruses and bacteria, our expectation of dramatic physical healing can be lowered, and we only really expect healing to take place following certain medical procedures. Furthermore, there is in our culture much cynicism and negativism, which is unbelief. I deal more fully with the stronghold of the Western worldview and the battle for healing in chapters 8 and 20 of my book *Demolishing Strongholds*.[1]

For this reason, we need to meditate regularly upon God's word concerning healing, and continue to pray and step out in faith based on God's word. There are two key scriptures among many others that we could refer to:

a) 'I tell you the truth, anyone who has faith in me will do what I have been doing. He will do even greater things than these, because I am going to the Father. And I will do whatever you ask in my name, so that the Son may bring glory to the Father. You may ask me for anything in my name, and I will do it.' (John 14:12–14)

One problem with our understanding of this scripture is that theologians and commentators have debated as to what exactly is meant by 'greater things'. Some would argue, for example, that the expression 'greater things' refers to conversion, which they say is greater than healing. This perspective has in itself caused people to back off from praying consistently for healing. However, we need to look at the context here. The context is the miracles that Jesus has been doing. Whatever 'greater things' may be, therefore, it is clear that Jesus intended us to do the 'things' (i.e. the miracles) that He was already doing. I personally believe that 'greater' refers to 'greater extent'. During His ministry on earth, Jesus was restricted to doing miracles in the towns of Palestine because He was limited to a physical body; now, however, He can work miracles through His church as His Holy Spirit is poured out upon believers everywhere.

b) 'Is any one of you in trouble? He should pray. Is anyone happy? Let him sing songs of praise. Is any one of you sick? He should call the elders of the church to pray over him and anoint him with oil in the name of the Lord. And the prayer offered in faith will make the sick person well; the Lord will raise him up. If he has sinned, he will be forgiven. Therefore confess your sins to each other and pray for each other so that you may be healed. The prayer of a righteous man is powerful and effective.' (James 5:13–16)

This scripture seems to describe an expectation of normal church life. If we are happy, we are to sing. If we are sick, we are to seek healing through the elders laying hands upon us and anointing us with oil. Incidentally, it is important again to see the biblical balance here. 'Gifts of healing' can be distributed widely within the body of Christ. We can therefore all pray for the sick. However, James teaches us that spiritual authority vested in the elders of the church is also to be used for healing. It is right, therefore, particularly when sickness has gone on for a while without being healed, for the person specifically to call in the elders of the church and for them to lay hands on the sick person and anoint them with oil.

3 Healing is to be seen as functioning within an atmosphere of loving care

We believe that God gives particular ministries of healing, but we are not to see healings as taking place only in the large 'healing meeting'. I do believe such meetings are important from time to time and that we should recognise those gifted as healing evangelists. However, when we go to one of these meetings, it is important that we look for our own faith to be extended and not just see it as a show, demonstrating somebody else's major gift. It is wonderful, too, on the occasions when we see such evangelists exercise demonstrable love and compassion to those they are praying for, as well as great faith for them to be healed.

It is important that the person being ministered to knows that we love them whatever the immediate prayer outcome.

Ongoing prayer is also important. We must also care for the sick, as well as praying for their healing, and this includes practical care for them and their families as an expression of the body of Christ. There are terminal illnesses from which people do not get healed and it is important that we minister the love of God to those in such conditions.

4 Getting to know the roots of an illness

As we have already seen, man is a unity and our minds, emotions, spirits and bodies are interconnected. Hence sickness can have different roots. This is recognised medically, where it is acknowledged that many sicknesses have psychosomatic roots. This does not mean that the sickness is not 'real' or that the pain does not exist. It is simply acknowledging that it may be brought on by other factors.

● Sometimes sickness can be the result of sin. Jesus refers to this by implication in John 5:14. This does not mean that all sickness is directly the result of sin by the person concerned or even by their family. Jesus again makes this clear in John 9:1–3. Of course, in general terms, all sickness is the result of sin having come into the world through the fall of man. However, we must not condemn people by blaming any sickness on some sin in their lives. On the other hand, we must not be afraid to confront sin if that is a current issue with them. Sins in emotional areas, such as bitterness, are important in this connection. It is noteworthy that in James 5:15–16, which we have already looked at, confessing our sins to one another is part of the healing process.

- Sickness may be rooted in emotional difficulties such as fear, insecurity, perfectionism, tension and stress.

- Sickness can sometimes be demonic in origin. In Jesus' time He identified 'spirits of infirmity' and is described by Peter as 'healing all who were under the power of the devil' (Acts 10:38).

- Sometimes we can identify real physical sickness as a result of a curse upon an individual or upon a family. This is more readily acknowledged in many Third World situations, but we do need to acknowledge it and set people free from curses.

  (Both these last two causes can include demonic effects on a family. Similarly, I have found that where there is strong domination and control within a family line, the effects may include sickness coming through the generations.)

- Excessive pressure of work.

- Overtiredness.

- Heredity factors.

- Functional discord, i.e. a purely physical cause which can be traced within the body or is the result of a physical accident.

How we pray can be determined by our discernment of the root. Also if sin, pressure of work or overtiredness is the genuine root cause, then we need to take specific action – that is, the person needs to repent of sin, seek to find a way of reducing pressure at work, and try and have more sleep.

When teaching on this particular issue, I often quote our own experience with our youngest daughter, Sharon. When she was about eighteen months old, I had been involved in praying for deliverance for somebody who was under a form of voodoo curse. I had actually been ministering to this person one particular evening, and then the next morning Sharon got out of her cot but could not walk. Her knee joints had swollen up very suddenly and eventually she was diagnosed at the hospital as having rheumatoid arthritis. We were told that this might be a juvenile form, which she would eventually grow out of, or it could be with her for the rest of her life. We obviously turned to prayer. We prayed publicly in our church and also set up a small group of ladies to pray regularly over her. They sometimes prayed when she was awake; they sometimes prayed when she was asleep. However, not only did they pray for her physical healing and for the effect of the counter-attack from the enemy, but they also prayed about certain emotions that my wife, Scilla, was feeling quite strongly when she was carrying Sharon in the womb. We had been going through a very difficult time in our church and a number of accusations had been made which had hurt Scilla deeply. Those praying therefore attacked three roots:

- a physical condition of rheumatoid arthritis

- demonic counter-attack

- emotional factors

Praise God, after a few sessions of prayer, the swelling went down, Sharon could walk easily again and the blood tests showed no rheumatoid factor in her blood.

5 Faith

Faith is often referred to in the Bible in the context of healing. 'Faith is the medium through which God releases His healing power' (John Wimber).[2]

Faith is almost always present when a healing takes place, but that faith can be operating in various people involved, for example:

- The sick person themselves. In Acts 14:9, for example, Paul saw that the crippled man had faith to be healed.

- Friends or relatives of the sick person. In Luke 5:20, Jesus healed a crippled man on seeing the faith of the four men who had brought him. In Luke 8:41, we find a father, Jairus, who had faith that Jesus could heal his daughter. On the other hand, sometimes relatives or close friends present when praying for healing can be a hindrance because they may create an overly emotionally charged atmosphere in which it is not faith that is present, but a burning desire to see the person get better. It may sometimes be necessary to ask them to withdraw while the praying takes place because faith can be hindered by such an emotional atmosphere.

- The person praying. It is the prayer of faith that can make the sick person well (James 5:15).

- Sometimes there can be general faith in a church or in a particular meeting because faith has been imparted by the teaching of the word of God on the subject of healing or by accurate words of knowledge, which reveal particular conditions that God is going to heal in that meeting.

- Faith is often simply the determination to step out. I have had the experience many times in public settings where I just know that God wants to demonstrate His healing power and so I step out in faith.

6 The prayer time

Various models and methods are used by different people who have a recognised healing ministry. For example, John Wimber gives a helpful outline of the 'Vineyard 5-stage model' in chapters 11 and 12 of his book *Power Healing*.[3] This gives some very helpful guidelines, but we must not be enslaved to one particular method.

a) Public prayer times

Currently, what I usually do is this:

i) I call people forward for specific conditions which I believe God has laid on my heart. This is not always a 'word of knowledge'. When large numbers of people are involved, it is very likely that there are going to be people with those conditions present. It is rather that when I have been praying prior to that meeting or during the worship time, I

sense particular conditions which God is going to heal on
those occasions.

ii) I then personally pray for each of these individuals myself.
In a smaller gathering, I may ask each one what they want
God to do for them and then leave them with a ministry-
team member for continued prayer as I move on to the
next person. In a large celebration meeting, I may just pray
over each person very briefly, without asking them any
questions first, and then encourage the ministry team to
continue praying. If the numbers were very large, I would
pray over the congregation from the front, with ministry-
team people standing with those who have come forward
for healing. Again the ministry team could then continue to
pray. Although by that time the Holy Spirit may have come
on the person in an outward way, we must not just look to
that for evidence of God moving. Often we find that God is
healing, without there being any outward manifestation.
We need to have a balance between a belief in 'every
member' ministry, so it is not just the preacher who is
anointed to pray, and a recognition of the anointing on the
speaker or leader and the help that his praying can give to
the sick person's faith.

iii) I would then call people forward, or ask them to stand up,
if they want prayer for healing for conditions that have not
been named. I would then proceed as above, though at that
time many of our ministry team may get involved in
initiating prayer, rather than just myself as the leader.

iv) The ministry team can be open to words of knowledge as to
why a person has that particular condition, but it is
important that we do not enter into long counselling in the
context of a ministry time like this. If the person being
prayed for needs to work through other issues, they need to
be referred to their local church leaders.

v) I believe it is right to follow the example of Jesus and others
in the New Testament and speak to the sickness at this
particular point. This is not the time for long intercession;
we should have done that before we came to the meeting!

Where there is an obvious external physical condition it can be helpful, as God prompts, to encourage people to do what they could not do before, e.g. to move their neck which was previously stiff or their shoulder which was previously 'frozen'. We also need to be open to different types of prayer for each person as we believe God directs – this is the prophetic dimension in the healing ministry.

b) Small, ministry-team situations

It is important that we set up small teams to pray for the sick and not just to concentrate on people's emotional problems. They need to consider the following points:

i) Ask the question 'What is wrong?' This does not mean a full medical analysis. To those untrained in medicine this can be confusing and can hinder rather than aid faith.

ii) As the person is speaking, we need to listen on two levels. On the one hand we are listening at the natural level and evaluating what they are saying in the light of our biblical knowledge and our experience. We are also, however, listening at the supernatural level and being open to God, to receiving words of knowledge, etc. However, it is important that we give the person our full attention because all this is an expression of our love to them.

iii) Examine why the person may have such a condition. It may not be what they think. I remember one situation where a bad back was traced to a physical accident, but actually the causes were both emotional and demonic. On that occasion, a hospital consultant recognised this as well and said to me that in this situation my methods were probably more useful than his. In this connection, people can suffer because of pronouncements by authority figures, which become self-fulfilling prophecies. For example, a doctor may be convinced that a person will not get better and tell them so. The doctor's well-intentioned words can then sometimes become an obstacle to faith for healing.

iv) There can be various types of prayer appropriate in different situations. We may have a surge of faith for a specific, one-off healing prayer. When we are praying over a longer period, intercession and standing before God for that person can be important. I would often encourage the person to pray for their own healing as well. It may be appropriate to pray concerning the emotional circumstances surrounding the problem if this is relevant. Sometimes we will speak words from God, again bringing the prophetic dimension into a small, ministry-team situation. There may be a word of command in a burst of faith, often accompanied by a sense of power and physical sensations. We may rebuke an evil spirit and speak to the condition.

This is not the place for long wordy prayers, trying to 'persuade' God to heal, but rather praying the words given us by God in faith that the Holy Spirit is leading us.

v) We may continue to ask questions:
- 'How are we doing?'
- 'Is it feeling better?'
- 'Is anything going on?'
- 'Is it worse?'

I find that sometimes people are afraid to ask these questions in case it diminishes their faith. However, I have known pain get worse before it gets better. There can be a battle involved.

vi) We need to give advice on what people should do to keep their healing or what to do if they are not healed. This may include:
- The importance of personal prayer and reading the Bible so that we concentrate on God and not our problems.
- The importance of fellowship in small groups and church.
- The importance of walking free of sin in our lives.
- Sometimes a change of environment may be appropriate if it is possible.
- We need to emphasise the need for commitment to one another and accountability.

If a person is not yet healed we may arrange further times of prayer.

Sometimes people are encouraged to have laying-on of hands on the area of the body that requires healing. This can be helpful but often it is not appropriate to do this when praying with a person of the opposite sex. If you are praying in teams, as I would advise, then have somebody of the same sex lay hands on the hurting part or let the sick person lay hands on themselves while you continue to pray.

7 Persistence

Some healing comes not as a result of one or two prayers but over a period of time. Francis McNutt devised the expression 'soaking prayer' for this. It includes:

- regular prayer times
- continuing to seek God for words which will help the situation
- praying into the surrounding circumstances or causes as God reveals them
- continuing to show love

8 Different ways in which God heals/ answers prayer

- Instantaneously. If this is in a public meeting and is so obvious as to need no medical verification, a testimony to what God has done can help others. Often, however, healing needs to be confirmed medically before a testimony is given, particularly as some symptoms do come and go. I would encourage people to go to the doctor if they are feeling better. There are well-attested cases of x-rays demonstrating the healing.

- Through a process. It is important that we continue to support the person in prayer.

- Spontaneously. This is where there has not been specific prayer beforehand but people are healed simply through the wonderful presence of God in a particular meeting. Kathryn Kuhlman often used to have words of knowledge in her meetings about conditions that were being healed at that moment. I have known situations where people have been spontaneously healed during the worship time and they find out afterwards.

- Through medical means. We are on the same side as the doctors in this respect. We believe that medicine is given as part of God's common grace to mankind. If we pray for someone to be healed and they then have an operation as a result of which they are healed, then we do not need to be ashamed of this. God has answered our prayer through medical means.

9 What about those who are not healed?

a) It is important that we never blame them for their lack of faith. We do not heap condemnation upon people.

b) Possible reasons for healing not taking place.

- Some people do not believe in healing for today. Although God may sovereignly overrule and heal despite their unbelief, it is unlikely that they will have great expectation or faith for healing.

- Sometimes personal unconfessed sin creates a blockage to healing. However, we must recognise that sometimes people can be wonderfully healed and never become Christians. I have seen this happen myself, and the story of the ten lepers in Luke 17:11–19 amply demonstrates it.

- Persistent and widespread disunity, sin and unbelief in companies of Christians can inhibit healing for individual members (1 Corinthians 11:30).

- There can be incomplete or incorrect diagnosis so that the root cause of the sickness is not dealt with.

- Sometimes there is a general negative attitude to life. It is hard to pray for hypochondriacs to be healed!

- Sometimes the person does not really want to be healed. They may think it is easier to stay as they are, or they may enjoy the attention they receive as a result of their condition. Even Jesus asked on one occasion 'Do you want to get well?' (John 5:6). I recall one incident where we were having prayer for healing at the end of a powerful church service and a particular man was encouraged to go forward. He protested and refused to do so because he said that if he were healed, he would have to get a job!

c) There is an element of mystery about physical healing. It has never been the experience of the church that all are healed. In John 5, even Jesus healed only one of a large number of people. We read about people having long-standing illnesses in the New Testament, even Christian leaders (1 Timothy 5:23; 2 Timothy 4:20). There is, for all, a time to die (Ecclesiastes 3:2). There are sicknesses which end in death, otherwise Jesus' words in John 11:4 to the contrary would not really have made sense.

I believe that the reason for this, theologically, is that although the kingdom of God has come, its fullness has 'not yet come'. The kingdom of God is here and therefore we expect to see people healed, but the kingdom of God has not yet come in all its fullness and will not do so until Jesus returns, when sickness, sorrow and death will be abolished. However, we have a responsibility to extend the kingdom here and now, and grow in faith. We therefore expect to see an increase in healing.

As we have said before, it is important that we care for the terminally ill and dying. This is an expression of the kingdom just as much as seeing prayer for healing answered.

10 Other miscellaneous points

a) It is important that we learn to see what God is doing. Jesus
said, 'I tell you the truth, the Son can do nothing by
himself; he can do only what he sees his Father doing,
because whatever the Father does, the Son also does' (John
5:19). He said this in the context of healing one particular
man out of a crowd. However, I would never refuse to pray
for somebody who comes for healing, although the
direction of that prayer must be subject to God's leading.
We need to learn to obey promptings of the Holy Spirit in
this as in other areas of our lives. Also, there do seem to be
particular seasons of power for healing, such as that
described in Luke 5:17.

b) Weak points. Many of us seem to have specific parts of our
bodies which are vulnerable to stress, tensions, emotional
problems and spiritual battles. It may appear therefore that
we 'lose our healing' in this respect. We need to be aware of
this and fight the root causes through spiritual warfare and
by walking in accordance with the word of God.

c) It is important that we live healthy lives as well as pray for
healing.

- We should take regular rest and relaxation and try to
avoid situations where rest and relaxation make us more
tense instead of better rested, such as going on holiday
with the in-laws!

- Our bodies need exercise, which in the sedentary
twenty-first century can be a problem for many of us.

- We should foster good eating habits with regular meals
and good food. However, we must not get legalistic.
There is a growing tendency in our Western world,
which has largely given up religion, to re-impose new
rules about what we should eat. White bread is not
holier than brown bread. Brown rice is not better for the
Christian than white rice. While recognising the virtues
of a healthy, balanced diet, we have to be careful that we
do not come under a new form of legalism which
attributes almost spiritual qualities to food.

- We need to learn how to cope in a godly way with stress and tension.

- We need to keep free of sin, including wrong anger, bitterness and resentment, as well as more obvious outward sins.

- We are created for community and therefore healing within relationships in the community, as we are sociable and friendly towards others, can also help physical healing.

- We need to remain in the love of God and not give way to self-rejection and condemnation or negative thinking.

[1] David Devenish, *Demolishing Strongholds*, Word UK 2000.
[2] John Wimber, *Power Healing*, Hodder & Stoughton 1986.
[3] *Ibid.*

Overcoming the Effects of Past Hurts

1 Introduction

a) The debate about 'inner healing'

There has been much debate among Christians in the last 20 years or so as to whether there is such a thing as 'inner healing', and among those who advocate it, there is a variety of definitions of it. It is instructive to examine some of these, to see what they offer to our understanding of this area of caring and healing.

i) David Seamands defined inner healing as 'ministering to and praying for damaged emotions and unhealed memories'.[1]

ii) Rita Bennett wrote, 'Inner healing is simply co-operating with the Lord to let him cure and remove from our psychological natures the things that are blocking the flow of the Holy Spirit.'[2]

iii) John Wimber defined inner healing as 'a process in which the Holy Spirit brings forgiveness of sins and emotional renewal to people suffering from damaged minds, wills and emotions'.[3]

The last of these definitions contains two elements that are missing from the others:

● forgiveness of sins

● the specific inclusion of mind and will as well as emotions

I believe we arrive at a more biblical position and avoid some of the dangers of looking at this subject unbiblically, if we take these two elements into account.

b) Definition

Healing past hurts is the application in practical terms of what is objectively true of every Christian in biblical terms: 'Therefore, if anyone is in Christ, he is a new creation; the old has gone, the new has come!' (2 Corinthians 5:17). Scripture presents us with another perspective in Colossians 3:1–14, where we read that although we are indeed 'new', we still have to 'put to death' what belongs to the old life, and 'clothe ourselves' with what belongs to the new. Therefore, if my reaction to past hurts is governing my behaviour now, it is part of the old that needs to be put off, so that I can put on the new. The fact that I am a new creature in Christ does not mean that I don't have to deal practically with the consequences of the past, where they are affecting the present.

It is possible for Christians to fail to live in the good of what Christ has done for them. Imagine that I inherited a castle in Scotland. I could go round to all my friends, telling them quite truthfully that I own a castle in Scotland, but if I never went to Scotland to stay at my castle and enjoy it, then even though I owned it, I would never enter into the good of it. And it is possible for us to do the same with our inheritance as Christians. It is true that we are a new creation in Christ; it is true that it is for freedom that Christ has set us free. But if we do not walk in newness and freedom, we are not entering into the inheritance that is there for us.

To take another example, Joshua was told, 'I will give you every place where you set your foot' (Joshua 1:3). Legally, the land belonged to the children of Israel already – God had promised it to them. But they had to enter into it in order to occupy it; they had to defeat the enemies who were there in order to enjoy their inheritance. The same is true for us: we have to defeat our enemies, some of which will be things pertaining to our past that stop us enjoying the inheritance of who we are in Christ. That is the true context of this ministry.

Jesus came to heal the broken-hearted (Isaiah 61:1) – those to whom dreadful things had happened (in today's language).

c) The purpose of dealing with the effects of past hurts

The objective of this ministry is that past sins and hurts should no longer govern present behaviour. Unfortunately, hurts that we have suffered and sins that we have committed in the past have affected our mind, emotions and spirit, and can govern our present behaviour. We need to find ways of applying God's truth to these so that they no longer govern the way we behave now, for we should be governed only by the lordship of Christ. Our memories may store up things that have happened to us, both facts and associated emotions. Our objective is to release the sting from the memory and the consequent emotional damage, so that these no longer govern the way we act. Note that accumulated hurts may come out in uncontrollable fits of jealousy and depression, and we may not be consciously aware of the pain.

This does not mean that every painful incident that has happened to us requires prayer; nor does it mean that everyone needs healing prayer. For example, if past rejection is preventing you from forming relationships now, the rejection needs dealing with. If, on the other hand, you have been rejected in the past, yet do not now have difficulty in relationships because of it, there is no need for healing prayer. Where the past is not governing present behaviour, leave well alone! There is no need to dig up and receive healing prayer for every unhappy memory – only those that continue to govern present behaviour.

Our objective is greater freedom in God's service and the extension of God's kingdom. This is not to make us 'feel better' nor to bring us to personal 'wholeness', which will not be attained until glory. It is to set us free to be recruited to play our full part in the army of God.

2 Understanding emotions

a) Feelings do matter!

It is a false worldview which says emotions are wrong or unimportant. God created emotions, and they are not something to be ashamed of, or wish we could do without. We

find the Bible full of people showing emotion. Jesus wept at
Lazarus's tomb (John 11:35) and showed anger in the temple
with the money-changers (John 2:15–17). The writers of the
Psalms and Lamentations expressed their depression and
anguish (e.g. Psalms 22; 42). Jesus told the story of the father
openly lavishing love and forgiveness on the prodigal son (Luke
15:20–24), rushing out to meet him, throwing his arms around
him, kissing him, ordering a feast for him.

b) The importance of expressing negative emotion

It is better to learn to acknowledge negative emotions rather
than deny them. Repressed hurts and emotions, such as fear,
anger, bitterness and jealousy, can lead to physical illness (for
example, ulcer, heart trouble, arthritis) and, conversely, physical
healing often results from emotional healing.

'Emotional and psychological hurts, including bad memories,
are caused both by our sin and by our being sinned against. The
healing of these past hurts restores the inward (unseen and
unseeable) part of men and women, as opposed to purely
physical, visible or outward healing' (John Wimber).[4]

c) Emotions are to be brought under the lordship of Christ

Our minds, for example, contain all sorts of wrong thoughts, but
we are to bring our thoughts captive into obedience to Christ
(2 Corinthians 10:5). Our actions, apart from Christ, are vain
and sinful, but we bring them under the lordship of Christ.
Similarly our emotions are not to be denied but expressed in an
appropriate way, under the lordship of Christ. So the Bible says,
for example, 'In your anger do not sin' (Ephesians 4:26).

d) We are created by God to have a number of sources of emotional health

i)   A sense of belonging. As we saw in Seminar 1, we were
     created for community, and it is not good for us to be
     alone. So if we are isolated or rejected, it has a negative
     emotional impact on us.

ii) A sense of value derived from being created in the image of God. If that is constantly undermined, for example by being told 'You're useless', it has a negative emotional impact on us.

iii) A sense of being able to do things. We need a sense of achievement, a sense that we can act effectively and bring about change in ourselves and our environment.

iv) A sense of felt love. Again, if we lack this sense of being loved, it may have a detrimental emotional effect on us.

3 Common emotional bondages

Each of the following could easily fill a whole chapter on its own, or even a whole book! In a work of this length and scope, it is inevitable that we shall skate over the surface to a large extent, but I hope at least to give clues and starting points for developing our understanding and finding our way into helping people with these sorts of difficulties. And we will possibly learn something about ourselves in the process!

a) Feeling useless

This is expressed most simply as 'I'm not good enough', 'I'm useless' or 'I'm hopeless'. Its origins may be:

i) Rejection by parents or other significant people. Rejection can take place before birth, as well as after it. I have had to deal with a number of people who were rejected in the womb, and there is some evidence of emotions being transmitted from the mother to the baby she is carrying. In ministering to people rejected before birth, it is important to have confirmatory evidence that the rejection took place. For example, a parent may have let slip that the child was unwanted, or the mother may be known to have considered an abortion. I once ministered to someone rejected before birth, who had been told by his parents that an illegal 'backstreet' abortion attempt had been made on him.

ii) Lack of approval and praise by parents, siblings, schoolteachers or peers. For example, a child may score

80% in a test, but instead of praise, Dad says, 'What about the other 20%?' Or a child passes an exam and hears only 'That's no more than you should have done.'

iii) Pressure to conform to false ideals. The 'image' of what the ideal man or woman ought to be so permeates our society that studies have shown even young children displaying symptoms of anorexia. Pressure to conform to false ideals comes through the constant bombardment of advertising and also through pressure from parents or peers who are themselves afflicted by it. So a slim mother constantly saying 'I'm too fat' may communicate to her child the idea that even the slightest chubbiness is undesirable. This pernicious falsehood dominates our culture and we need to stand firm in repudiating it.

iv) Guilt over a grievous sin, or a sin we regard as particularly grievous. We may have difficulty in accepting God's forgiveness, or in forgiving ourselves. We may have a heightened view of the seriousness of a particular sin we have committed, as against sins committed by other people. All sin is wrong, but it is possible to get our own sin, or one particular sin, out of proportion.

v) Words that bind. For example, 'You'll never be any good at that.' We have already looked at this in Seminar 3 above.

The one talent man in Matthew 25:14–30 presents us with a good example of a sense of unworthiness. He was filled with the fear of rejection because he misunderstood what his master was really like; he had a fear of failure and so did not use his one talent at all; and he had a fear of comparison with the successful people.

b) Perfectionism

I call this 'the bondage of the oughts'. 'You ought to keep the house cleaner, you ought to have time for this, you ought to do that...' The tape plays on inside your head, and you never feel you have done as well as you ought.

The origins of perfectionism may be:

i) Rejection. This is almost the converse of the effect of rejection above. Instead of driving us into a sense of defeated unworthiness, rejection can lead us into constantly trying to prove ourselves, and thus we become perfectionists.

ii) Lack of approval. 'You should have done better' can drive us into perfectionism as well as into unworthiness.

iii) Inherited perfectionism. It is common to find a person trying to live up to the same unrealistic high standards their parents had. 'My mother dusted the coal...'

iv) Religious legalism. This can be particularly powerful when added to the other things, as it often is.

Though perfectionists usually maintain a calm exterior (because they feel they ought to!), they usually have real anger underneath, often expressed against others who don't conform to the 'oughts' and who are relaxed and happy in not doing so.

Perfectionism can have two consequences:

i) Breakaway. This is when we give up, because we believe we cannot do anything properly, nor can anyone else. People can even backslide from faith because they become disillusioned with their own lack of perfection and that of the church.

ii) Breakdown, usually through workaholism.

c) Supersensitivity

Supersensitive people are very easily hurt. They are the sort of people who take offence very easily and require extremely careful handling. Its origins may be:

i) Rejection. Rejection is a very powerful and common cause of hurt because it is a primary characteristic of Satan. He is a rejected being, and rejection rules in his kingdom – the exact opposite of the acceptance which characterises the kingdom of God.

ii) Trauma. This can be a bad experience such as seeing death, or even watching violence on TV as children. A scene in which a child is hurt can have a worse effect than something more obviously 'scary', such as monsters.

iii) A lot of shouting or unpredictability in the home. This may include parental inconsistency such as punishing harshly an offence that was only laughed at the day before.

iv) Violence in the home, such as frequent beatings or a drunken father.

People who are very prickly often set up barriers to stop you getting too close to them, and may put your acceptance and love for them to the test before they allow you any closer. They may, for example, fail to keep an appointment, or say something nasty to you, to see whether you are going to reject them. They fear that if they allowed you to come close enough to get inside their emotional barriers, to the place where they began to trust you, you might reject them, which they would be unable to cope with. So they prefer to keep you at a safe distance where they still feel in control and where any pain, if you do hurt them, will be minimised and more remote.

d) Fear

It is surprising how many Christians are gripped by fear. Its origins may be:

i)   Trauma.

ii) Inherited fear. If, for example, your mother was always afraid of thunderstorms, you may be afraid of them too.

iii) Occultism and superstition in the family or earlier in life. Superstitions breed fear because they are an attempt to predict or influence future events, and to bring order to an environment perceived to be hostile or capricious.

iv) Unpredictability in the home.

e) Sexual problems: frigidity or fear of sex

Its origins may be:

i)   Sexual abuse as a child.

ii) Sexual sin in the family tree.

iii) A home background in which sex is regarded as wrong or unmentionable. This may have a religious element to it.

iv) Other emotional problems as mentioned above.

v)   Promiscuity before marriage or a lack of courtship. People who have been promiscuous before marriage or have slept together very early in their relationship can find they have difficulties in maintaining a satisfying sexual relationship once they are married. There is usually a lack of understanding that the sexual relationship should be the expression of the full commitment made in marriage, and that courtship is the preparation for this. It would be easy to imagine that a couple with wide sexual experience would have no problems in this area, but in fact the opposite is often true.

Promiscuity can result from any of the above (i–iv). It seems that abuse and similar problems can result either in a fear of sex, or in a sense of worthlessness which leads to the attitude of 'My body's not worth anything, so I'll give it to anybody'.

f) Sexual problems: homosexuality

It is almost impossible to address this in a paragraph or two. The following gives only the beginning of a lead into this complex area, and it would be helpful to read further on the subject, particularly the writings of the Christian psychiatrist Elizabeth Moberly,[5] and Frank Worthen's *Steps Out of Homosexuality* (Love in Action).[6]

The origins of homosexuality are often:

i)   The inability to form a good relationship with an important male, such as a father, early in life. The father may not be to blame for this, but may be unavoidably absent. This lack of relationship with a significant male leads to the seeking

of male affection to fill the gap, which later becomes
sexualised. Elizabeth Moberly suggests that this is a major
origin of homosexuality.

ii) A domineering mother, who inhibits her son from learning
as a boy how to relate to others as males.

iii) Sexual abuse as a boy by a man or by another boy. The
victim usually experiences homosexual feelings but, at the
same time, hates those feelings. He may hate taking part in
homosexual acts and yet feel driven to experiment.

iv) Rejection in a heterosexual relationship.

Dealing with the sexual problem of homosexuality invariably
needs more than just ministry sessions. It requires a reorienta-
tion of thought life and relationships by building good, open
and accountable relationships in the body of Christ.

g) Sexual problems: lesbianism

Its origins are often:

i) Infantile deprivation. In other words, a lack of care and
affection from the mother when young.

ii) A possessive and domineering mother. A possessive,
devouring love is easily sexualised.

iii) Estranged femininity. This is a lack of clear sexual identity
as a female. It may be the result of parents wanting a boy
rather than a girl, and failing to encourage their daughter to
develop her femininity. A father may treat his daughter as if
she were a boy.

iv) A fear or hatred of one's father or other men.

v) It is suggested that it is often an emotional dependency that
will arise first in lesbian relationships which, as it develops,
may be sexualised. Two needy people can use each other's
needs to develop an unhealthy, dependent relationship
which can easily become sexualised. The same can happen
even within a counselling relationship, where a strong,
dominant counsellor and a lonely, needy counsellee develop
a dependency relationship which then becomes sexualised.

h) Rebellion

In one sense we are all rebellious, for rebellion is the essence of sin. Nonetheless, in seeking to bring healing, we need to keep certain specific origins in mind.

i) Anger at a lack of 'fences' when a child. Children need fences, i.e. clearly defined borders between what is right and what is wrong, what is permitted and what is forbidden. If they don't have such fences, they tend to rebel to try and establish what and where the fences should be.

ii) Rejection. When someone has problems with both rejection and rebellion, they can prove very difficult to counsel. When we show acceptance and love towards them they rebel against it, and when we confront the rebellion they interpret the correction as rejection.

iii) Starvation of physical love and its opposite, an over-protective upbringing. In a sense, parents cannot win! It is hard to find the middle course between the two extremes of a stifling, over-protective love and a casual, laissez-faire love, either of which can lead to a child rebelling.

i) Conclusion

Each of these damaged emotions may have accompanying demons, but this is not necessarily so or usually so. When these problems are being ministered to, there may be shaking, contortions and other similar symptoms, which are simply expressions of emotion, and are not necessarily demonic. If we are praying about breaking the power of rejection in someone's life, this does not mean we are expelling a spirit of rejection. I usually explain this by saying, 'I'm going to break the power of rejection in your life. This doesn't mean there's a demon there.' But I also go on to say that sometimes the healing prayer brings to light a demon which has got hold of the emotional disturbance so that there can be, for example, a spirit of rejection there.

Please remember that although we may correctly diagnose the origins of an emotion, that does *not* excuse us from personal responsibility for that emotion. For example, we may find out the origins of a person's sense of unworthiness. Unworthiness is actually a form of self-rejection, of rejecting what God has created. That is sin, and must be acknowledged as such and repented of and confessed, whatever its origin. The circumstances of a problem's origins do not excuse our sinful reaction to those circumstances.

4 How do we lead a hurt person to open up?

a) It is essential to show love, acceptance and concern. It may take a long time to build up trust where people have a crushed spirit (Proverbs 15:13; 17:22; 18:14) which affects their physical, emotional and spiritual well-being. So before starting healing prayer, it may be appropriate to encourage the person to put themselves in a place where they can find acceptance and begin to learn to trust and open up a bit. They may need to spend time with you or with other Christians and begin to build friendships and find acceptance in normal, everyday situations, rather than just in the rarefied atmosphere of 'healing prayer'.

b) Watch out for and respond to tell-tale signs, the signals that hurting people send out unconsciously, that let you know they are in difficulties. These can be used manipulatively, so take care! Watch out for:

   i)   subtle hints;

   ii) a sad or downcast expression;

   iii) uncharacteristic behaviour, particularly uncharacteristic indecisiveness;

   iv) letting routine tasks go, which is often a sign of depression. This can include a lack of care about personal appearance, grooming and cleanliness;

   v)   body language (see Seminar 3);

   vi) drug addiction or alcoholism.

   Respond with great care when you see any of these signs. A person suffering rejection may react strongly when they first find acceptance.

c) Look out for trigger events. A seemingly trivial remark or event may 'trigger' a strong reaction from a hurting person. You may do or say something apparently harmless, which provokes a strong outburst of anger or rejection that seems out of all proportion to the situation. When this happens, do not worry about what you have said or done. The person is reacting to a much deeper pain which you have unwittingly touched or 'triggered'. Simply apologise, and then look past the surface issue and try to minister to the deeper problem.

5. Once the person has begun to open up

a) Continue to show acceptance. Since a rejected person expects to be rejected, they may pre-empt the expected rejection by trying to make you reject them. This may be a behaviour pattern they are largely unconscious of, or it may be a deliberate attempt to retain control of the relationship, so that if it fails, they can say to themselves 'I made them reject me' rather than endure the helplessness and humiliation of being rejected again.

b) Be open to pictures, words of knowledge, etc. as you minister to the person. They may hide the real reason for their pain, and the Holy Spirit may give you revelation on this. See the section on 'Using spiritual gifts' in Seminar 1 above.

c) Sometimes there may be more than one problem. It can be like peeling an onion layer by layer; as one problem comes to the surface and is dealt with, it reveals another underneath. Or we might look at it as 'opening a can of worms'. We need to be prepared to deal with each problem, or 'worm', as it emerges. This can take time, but it is important that it is seen in the context of helping someone forward in their discipleship and not as digging around in their subconscious.

d) Make sure that ministry to one problem is secure before tackling the next. When one emotional issue has been dealt with, there is no excuse for the person to go back on what has been done, just because another emotional problem has come to the surface. Ensure that ministry to a previous problem(s) is being 'stood on' firmly, or you can go round in circles from one problem to another, resolving nothing. As stated above, this can take some time, particularly when a person is very damaged. Each time we pray for the Holy Spirit to come, some reaction may occur. This can be hysterical or 'put on', and we need to look for real progress in the person's discipleship.

e) Allow for expression of pain. In severe cases of abuse and other serious emotional damage, time needs to be taken for 'memory work'. When something terrible has happened to someone and is obviously governing their present behaviour and emotions, they may be unable to speak about it. This silence gives the past events power over the person's life. Once they start to talk about it, it helps release them from the power of what has happened to them. Memory work is an important part of the healing process. It will involve a lot of pain and anger coming out. Once all their pain is expressed, do not leave them there, but bring them through to release and peace.

6 Methodology: values and principles

Inner healing has become widely practised in the charismatic renewal, and most has not been very biblical, in my opinion. It can be dangerous to develop a particular model or method perhaps based on a technique that proved successful in one particular situation, and may indeed have been prophetic and God-given for that situation. It is not wise or helpful to take a method that worked well once and set it up as a model for other situations. Rather, we should base our work on biblical values and principles, and an openness to the direction of the Holy Spirit in each individual case.

a) The individual's responsibility

Remember that the objective is to bring a person to accept responsibility for their past actions, so that they can act responsibly in the future without being subject to bondage from the past. The fact that sin may have certain origins does not excuse it.

b) Applying biblical truth

Many problems will be dealt with by a simple application of what God says in His word. For example, we all have value because we are:

- created by God (Psalm 139:13–18)
- chosen by God (Ephesians 1:4)
- loved and redeemed by Him (Galatians 2:20)
- blessed by Him (Ephesians 1:3)

We need to speak God's word prophetically and prayerfully to people. Even if we have to take more time, we must still keep applying the word of God, the sword of the Spirit. A lot of the apparent need for such ministry arises from the fact that the mind has been programmed to think negatively and needs to be renewed (Romans 12:2). A perfectionist, for example, needs to take on board the truth of God's grace, both for themselves and towards other people.

c) Forgiveness

Forgiveness is the key to the healing of the emotions. Its importance cannot be stressed too much.

What is forgiveness?

Forgiveness is not pretending that the offence never took place, or that it was less serious than it really was, or that it does not matter.

Forgiveness is:

i) Taking the offence seriously, giving it its true value and acknowledging the pain it has caused.

ii) Letting the other person off the hook completely, setting your will to never again hold that offence against them, and holding to that decision whenever your emotions bring it all up again.

iii) Agreeing to bear the cost of what they did and not go for revenge or repayment of the debt. In fact, we will have to bear the cost of what was done against us, no matter what, since there is no way of undoing the past. Our only choice is whether to bear it in the freedom of forgiveness or the bondage of bitterness.

iv) An act of the will, not of the emotions, deciding to forgive in obedience to Christ because He has forgiven us (Colossians 3:13).

Why is it so important to forgive?

i)   Healing of past hurts is not intended to excuse us from responsibility, but to enable us to take proper responsibility for our reactions to hurt. And the only true Christian reaction to hurt is to forgive (Matthew 18:21–22; Luke 23:34; Acts 7:60).

ii) If we do not forgive, we are effectively 'in prison'. Jesus told the parable of the unmerciful servant in direct response to Peter's question about forgiveness, and ends it with the sobering warning: 'His master turned him over to the jailers to be tortured … This is how my heavenly Father will treat each of you unless you forgive your brother from your heart' (Matthew 18:34–35).

iii) If we do not forgive, we harbour hidden anger and resentment, which give a foothold for the devil (Ephesians 4:26–27). Forgiveness releases the negative emotions of anger, resentment and bitterness, and demolishes any hold the devil may have in our emotions. When forgiveness has taken place it is therefore possible to drive out any spirits which have attached themselves to the anger.

iv) If we do not forgive, we may be failing to acknowledge that the other person has sinned and hurt us. Thus we are in practice blaming ourselves, or at least directing all our anger against ourselves rather than against the other person. We are effectively saying that we are to blame, and thus failing to enjoy the forgiveness of God. This heartache leads to us having a crushed spirit (Proverbs 15:13), and a sense of oppression and self-rejection. If somebody has sinned against us, we need to place the blame where it belongs and then release the other person from blame, and ourselves from oppression and bitterness, by forgiving them.

How does forgiveness take place?

i)   We need to receive God's forgiveness for our own sins in the matter, in response to our repentance. For example, we can repent of self-rejection, of rejecting what God has created. We must confess and accept forgiveness for both current sins and past sins that are still binding us. And in so doing, we need to forgive ourselves. We need to accept God's word concerning both our guilt and the forgiveness He has promised when we repent and confess our sins (1 John 1:8–9).

ii) We need to forgive the people who have hurt us, however awful they may have been. For example, we may need to forgive parents for beating and rejecting us, peers for bullying us at school, a husband or wife for being unfaithful. In cases of sexual assault, we need to forgive the person who did it.

iii) Often there is deep anger against God or against others. This needs to be confessed. I have heard cases of people being counselled to 'forgive' God when they perceive Him to be responsible for their pain. This is wrong and, in fact, blasphemous, because God does not sin and therefore stands in no need of our forgiveness! We can express our anger and pain to Him – the Psalms are full of such expression, as we have seen – but we are to submit to God, not set ourselves up to judge Him as being at fault. We must also repent of anger against God.

iv) Forgiveness is not cheap. It can cost us dearly, and there is often a great struggle, with strong emotions coming out, evidenced by shaking, screaming or anger.

v)   We need to try and be sure that forgiveness has really taken place, and the person is not just saying empty words, or evading the issue by saying 'I want to forgive...' or 'God, help me to forgive...' rather than actually saying 'I forgive...'.

vi) Healing of the emotions can be received once forgiveness has taken place, and we need to pray for the person's healing at this point.

d) Cutting the emotional/spiritual umbilical cord

Very often, people have not been emotionally released by their parents. Sometimes this is because the parents remain possessive of their adult children; sometimes the person still feels in bondage to their parents, e.g. in need of their approval or fearful of their rejection. There can also be inherited emotional problems or demonisation in the family tree (see Seminar 6 below).

People need to be cut off from this emotional umbilical cord in Jesus' name, on the basis of their identity and freedom in Christ.

i)   Every Christian is a new creation under new management; the old has gone and the new has come (2 Corinthians 5:17).

ii) A married adult has left their parents' home and the parents no longer have authority over them (Genesis 2:24).

iii) A single adult is equally free of parental control as Jesus demonstrated when, as a single man, He stood firm against His mother's and brothers' attempts to take Him in hand (Mark 3:20–21, 31–34).

iv) This does not mean that we should not love and honour our parents. Jesus' care for Mary is exemplary, as He thought of her and committed her to John's protection in His dying moments on the cross (John 19:26–27).

Parents may have to be led to cut the emotional cord by which they are still holding on to their own now grown-up children.

e) Christ as High Priest

Christ Himself suffered and can therefore sympathise with and enter into our sufferings (Hebrews 4:15; 5:7–8). He suffered:

- the stigma of illegitimacy
- rejection by establishment
- rejection by family
- rejection by friends
- rejection by God – so that we may never be rejected
- lies about Himself

It is often helpful to apply these truths to a hurting person.

f) Other techniques used by some in this ministry

i) Visualisation. Some practitioners use the visualisation technique of the person being led to see Jesus appear in the situation which hurt them, bringing love and healing. Others go to the extreme of leading the person to visualise Jesus appearing and changing the course of events as if the painful experience never happened.

There are a number of objections to this procedure:

- We cannot change history. What has happened has happened and must be dealt with in reality.
- Visualisations of this kind can lead people to adopt a distorted mental picture of Christ and His character.
- The technique is vulnerable to manipulation, which can become occultic.
- It can result in avoidance of responsibility for our reactions to real past events.

ii) The causing of feelings to be expressed. This often happens in any case as people revisit their painful memories. Sometimes it is necessary to bring the person face to face with their real emotion, which they may previously have felt unable to acknowledge. For example, someone who has been hurt by a close family member may feel it is not acceptable to admit to feeling anger or hatred towards them. It is good to encourage them to acknowledge such negative emotions, not because it is right to hate one's brother, but because the truth needs to be faced! And once those emotions are acknowledged, it becomes possible to deal with them through repentance.

iii) Beware of mysticism. By that, I mean any philosophy or practice that separates mystical spiritual experiences from real life. For example, beware of leading somebody to experience wonderful light, or 'being slain in the Spirit', without teaching them to cease from sin.

g) Aftercare

i) It is essential for the person who has received healing prayer to continue in Christian fellowship, care and friendship. Good friendships are particularly important so that the person does not develop an unhealthy dependence on those who have counselled them, but learns how to make and maintain friendships themselves.

ii) They will also need to be taught how to stand firm on the progress they have made and the truths that have been applied to their lives. They need to know how to avoid the dangers of Satan tempting them again. For example, a person who has suffered from rejection will need to learn how to cope when someone rejects, or appears to reject, them in the future. They must also learn to forgive others immediately.

[1] David Seamands, *Healing For Damaged Emotions*, Victor Books 1981.
[2] Rita Bennett, *How to Pray for Inner Healing*, Fleming H. Revell 1984.
[3] John Wimber, *Power Healing*, Hodder & Stoughton 1986.
[4] *Ibid.*
[5] Elizabeth Moberly, *Homosexuality, A New Christian Ethic*, James Clarke & Co 1983.
[6] Frank Worthen, *Steps Out of Homosexuality*, Love in Action 1985.

Healing the Demonised

1 Biblical background

The issue of setting people free from demonic power can be somewhat controversial within the Christian church. There is not time to go into all the controversy in a course like this. However, it is important that you understand on what assumptions the course is based and these therefore need to be set out at the beginning of this chapter.

a) Demons exist. They are evil, malevolent spirits with personality. They are under the direction of Satan and can inhabit people and occasionally places. (For example, I have sometimes been asked to pray around houses where there seems to be some evil presence.)

b) A number of expressions are used in Scripture to describe the effect of demons upon people's lives. They are:

- Being demonised. This means being affected by or under the influence of a demon to a greater or lesser extent. Scriptures include Matthew 4:24; 8:16, 28, 33; 9:32; 12:22; 15:22; Mark 1:32; 5:5, 16, 18; Luke 8:36; John 10:21.

- Having demons (Luke 8:27)
  a dumb spirit (Mark 9:17)
  unclean spirits (Mark 1:23; 5:2; 7:25; Acts 8:7AV)
  a spirit of an unclean demon (Luke 4:33AV)
  a spirit of infirmity (Luke 13:11AV).

- Being troubled by spirits (Luke 6:18).
- Being afflicted by spirits (Acts 5:16NAS).
- Having seizures (Luke 9:39).
- Being entered into (Luke 8:30; 22:3; John 13:27).
- Being filled (by Satan) (Acts 5:3 – same word as filled by the Holy Spirit).

Nowhere is the word 'possessed' used in the original Greek.
This word tends to be frightening and suggests total control
and ownership. It is commonly used in our translations for
'demonised', but I prefer not to use it. I prefer to talk of
severe or mild demonisation. For example, one demonised
man could be naked and in the tombs, cutting himself with
stones. Another demonised man could be in the synagogue
taking part in the worship normally until Jesus entered.
One is an example of severe demonisation, and the other of
mild demonisation.

c) I believe a Christian can be demonised and therefore can be
set free from the effect of those demons working in their
life. I believe this for the following reasons:

- Scripture describes the phenomenon of demons being
  cast out or evidently coming out.

- If such demons have not been cast out, how have they
  gone? I would suggest that Scripture gives no warrant for
  demons automatically disappearing. We are told to heal
  the sick, cast out demons, preach the gospel. If the gospel
  is preached without healing the sick, the sick remain
  sick. So also, in my view, if the gospel is preached
  without casting out demons, then the demonised
  usually remain demonised until the demons are cast out.

- What about those who are 'Spirit-filled'? Can they be
  demonised? I believe we can misunderstand what 'Spirit-
  filled' means. Sometimes we use the analogy of a glass of
  water and assume that being filled with the Holy Spirit
  means being full as the glass is full of water. There is
  then no room for anything else. A better analogy of the
  dynamic filling of the Holy Spirit is the way in which
  the wind fills a sail. It is dynamic action.

- People of faith and those who had previously been filled
  by the Spirit were or became demonised. King Saul in
  the Old Testament had been filled with the Holy Spirit
  and had prophesied, yet he was later afflicted by an evil
  spirit. The woman with the curved spine in Luke 13:11
  is described as a 'daughter of Abraham'. I would suggest

this means she was a person of faith, yet she was afflicted by a spirit of infirmity.

- There are references in Scripture to our giving a foothold to the devil if we hold on to anger or do not forgive, e.g. Matthew 18:34–35; Ephesians 4:27. The devil cannot be omnipresent. The devil works through demons, and giving footholds to the devil could well mean giving footholds to demonic power to work in our lives.

- The story of the Canaanite woman (Matthew 15:26) tells of her seeking deliverance for the daughter. Jesus said that is was not right to take 'the children's bread' and give it to the dogs. It would seem that Jesus meant that deliverance was 'the children's bread'. If deliverance is staple food for God's children according to Jesus, then it would suggest that deliverance is generally more effective in the lives of believers than of those who are not.

This subject is considered in more detail in chapter 7 of my book *Demolishing Strongholds*.

d) Demons are at work in various ways:

- To tempt us (though not all temptation is demon induced – it is sometimes just our flesh).
- To oppose or attack us.
- Through demonisation. This is where demons get a grip to a greater or lesser extent on people's personalities or physical bodies, producing bondages and patterns of temptation and weakness that are not changed by repentance.

We can all be affected by the first two of these influences and need to resist the devil and submit to God. With demonisation, however, the demons need to be cast out.

e) We need to be careful about our language. What do we mean when we say 'a spirit of...'? We can sometimes say that somebody has a 'spirit of fear' or 'a spirit of lust', when we really mean that they are very fearful or are often subject to the temptation of lust. This does not necessarily denote the presence of a demon. Sometimes we talk about a 'spirit of heaviness' in a particular meeting. This could simply be that people are feeling lethargic that morning. It may not be anything to do with evil spirits!

2 How do people become demonised?

Here we are looking at entry points for demons into somebody's life. Although it is not always necessary to identify the entry point in order to cast the demon out, it is often useful to do so in order to help the person concerned walk free of the issue once they have been set free.

a) Sin. Saul's rebellion is described as being like the sin of witchcraft (1 Samuel 15:23). This led to him having an evil spirit (1 Samuel 16:14). It is important to note the symptoms of this – fits of anger, murder, fear, witchcraft and eventually suicide. It was not that Saul got involved with witchcraft and therefore had an evil spirit; it was rather that he had an evil spirit because of his sin, which eventually led him to witchcraft. Other sins which often give access to evil spirits include: unrighteous anger, self-hatred, intense hatred of others, strong desires for revenge, unforgiveness, pornography, sexual wrongdoing, perversions and abortion. I have noticed that in the case of abortion, it is not just the woman involved but others involved in the decision who may be adversely affected.

b) Occult involvement and Eastern religions. This might include the following:

   • Fortune-telling: ouija boards, tarot cards and any other kind of fortune-telling such as tea leaves, palmistry or a crystal ball.

   • Spiritualism: horoscopes, so-called Christian spiritualism, séances and mediums, automatic writing, spiritualist healing and clairvoyance.

   • Magic: black and white magic, table-lifting, levitation, casting spells and hexes.

   • Mysticism: transcendental meditation, astral projection, mind-reading, mental telepathy, thought transference and mind-expanding drugs.

- Freemasonry.
- Religions: Satanism, idol worship.

c) Traumatic experiences, i.e. sins against us. This includes sexual abuse as children, rape and severe rejection by parents or others.

d) Curses or witchcraft against somebody. A lot of this may simply relate to demonic attack. We must not presume that curses against us will stand. Indeed, Proverbs 26:2 encourages us to think otherwise. However, it is possible for believers to give a curse a resting place through sin or their emotions.

3 Symptoms of demonisation

The presence of one or more of the following symptoms indicates the possibility, though not the necessity, that a person is demonised. Often people who claim they are demonised are not. It is important when going through a list like this that we do not give way to fear. It can rather be like going through a family health guide and as a result thinking we have got half the infectious diseases mentioned!

- Unpleasant contorted physical reactions, especially when the power of the Holy Spirit is evidently present.

- Addiction to drugs or alcohol.

- A problem with compulsions. By compulsions I mean not just idle thoughts or occasional temptations but rather a strong vortex into which we seem to be frequently drawn involving these things. They include lust, fornication and sleeping around, pornography, compulsive masturbation, homosexuality, habitual stealing, thoughts of murder, habitual lying, constant suicidal thoughts and possibly sometimes eating disorders. As we have said elsewhere in this course, some of these issues need longer-term help for us to walk free, but they can suggest the possibility of demonic involvement.

- A bondage to emotions such as fear, constant depression, anxiety and uncontrollable rage.

- A bondage to sinful attitudes like self-hatred, unforgiveness, bitterness and resentment.

- Sometimes (though this is not always true) chronic physical sicknesses, especially sicknesses that have been in the family for several generations without any obvious reason.

- A history of occult involvement as described in the earlier section.

- A disturbed family history involving, for example, incest, alcoholism and various forms of child abuse.

- Symptoms of rejection. Rejection is one of Satan's strongest weapons. Deep rejection could simply be an issue of our emotions but is sometimes demonic. These symptoms include:
    an inability to feel love;
    an innate mistrust of people;
    an inability to form any lasting relationships;
    a persecution complex;
    irrational frustrations and anger;
    an inability to receive correction because correction is
        misinterpreted as rejection.

- Symptoms of self-rejection (which again could be emotional but could also involve the demonic):
    deep lack of value as created in the image of God;
    negative about everything concerning oneself;
    lack of self-care;
    thoughts of suicide.

Incidentally, I have found that the following problems often run together where we are dealing with demonic power in this context:
    rejection;
    self-rejection;
    fear of rejection;
    rejecting of others.

- Exceptional parental dominance, which we find it very difficult to get free from. Again, this is covered in more detail in chapter 12 of *Demolishing Strongholds*.

- 'Soul-ties.' These are unhealthy ties that have arisen from a very close relationship with an emotionally disturbed or demonised person, or a wrong sexual relationship with such a person. People who have slept around a lot before they come to Christ may have soul-ties because the act of sexual intercourse is not only a physical thing, as Scripture makes clear (1 Corinthians 6:12–19).

- 'Religious spirits.' Those who have been brought up in a very legalistic or superstitious religious system – even if it is Christian – can be in bondage to these spirits. There are 'deceiving spirits' involved in legalistic, superstitious or excessively ritualistic forms of Christianity and in the cults (see 1 Timothy 4:1–5).

4 Preparation for ministry

Deliverance is an authority issue and, while I do not believe that elders and pastors should do all the deliverance ministry, I do believe that they should only give such responsibility to those in whom they have confidence. It is very important that anyone working in this field is rightly related to godly authority in their local church.

Sometimes a demon will manifest in a person's life, either in a church meeting or when we are praying with them for something else. Obviously there is not then time to go and prepare ourselves properly – we just have to get on with it. However, if we know we are going to be involved in a deliverance situation, then some preparation is helpful.

- Worship. It is important to honour Jesus. His is the name above every name, at which demons have to flee. Worship can be both on our own and with the team with whom we will be ministering.

- Prayer. It is good to have a prayer base. Jesus said on one occasion in relation to a deliverance situation, 'This kind can come out only by prayer' (Mark 9:29). Here I think He was referring primarily to the disciples' general prayer life.

Nevertheless, special seasons of prayer and supporting prayer groups may be necessary in very difficult deliverance situations. Sometimes we encounter people who have been very heavily involved in occult or even Satan worship, or who have had very deep problems and received ministry many times, but who do not seem to be free. These are the sort of situations where special supporting prayer groups may be necessary.

- Always pray in a team of at least two. For severe demonisation, perhaps one or two more people may be appropriately added.

- Remind yourself of your own authority in Christ. It is important to remember that we are raised up and seated with Him in heavenly places. We can overcome Satan by the blood of the Lamb and the word of our testimony (Revelation 12:11). We are commissioned by Christ to set people free. Demons have no right to be among us and therefore should be expelled from the life of a believer.

- Seek God for the gift of discernment of spirits and for words of knowledge that may be relevant to that situation. The gift of discernment of spirits is the God-given ability to distinguish whether the origin of feelings, words and actions is divine, human or demonic. It is also important to seek God for discernment to know when a demon has gone. Though sometimes this is obvious, it is not always the case immediately. Sometimes any outward manifestations may stop, but the demon has not actually gone and is hiding.

- Seek to be filled again with the Holy Spirit and confess and receive forgiveness for any sin in your own life. I have found in deliverance ministry that this is particularly important in the realm of relationships. If we are harbouring unforgiveness towards somebody who has hurt us, then, as with any other sin, Satan the accuser can remind us of it when we are involved with seeking to set somebody free. Sometimes, indeed, the enemy seeks to bring disruption in relationships, e.g. between a husband and wife, just before one of them is to be involved in deliverance ministry.

- It is important that those praying fix the time of ministry if at all possible. Do not let the demonised person call the shots. Sometimes they seek to gain your attention at inappropriate times. We can sometimes be pressurised because somebody believes that if they have a demon it must be got rid of immediately. We need to remember (though it is not pastorally sensitive to say this!) that sometimes those demons have been in the person's life for many years and a few days is not going to make a lot of difference.

- When praying in these circumstances, try to be private and in a quiet, relatively soundproof place! Normally we use our church building, but I know that is not possible for those who lack such a facility. However, it is not helpful to start praying in this way in the midst of a crowded family home, perhaps with the children around, and no privacy.

5 The deliverance procedure

- Since, as I have said, deliverance is an authority issue, be sure that you are working together as a team with one recognised leader to whom the rest of the team submit. In severe cases of demonisation, it is advisable to have somebody involved who is experienced and has pastoral authority. It is best to decide beforehand who the team leader should be and, during ministry, it is important that you do not all crowd round the person, talking at the same time, commanding the demon to go. There is no need for more than one person to speak at once.

- Put the person at ease and take any mystery or perceived 'spookiness' out of the situation. Explain from Scripture the truth concerning their situation. During this preliminary conversation, it is important to ascertain whether the person really wants to be set free and live a life very different from what may have governed them hitherto.

- As we move into the time of ministry, it is important first of all to pray, inviting the presence of the Holy Spirit into the situation.

- The person we are ministering to now needs to repent of sin and renounce evil. Repentance involves getting rid of any footholds the devil may have, by turning away from any known sin in their life. This includes personal involvement in the occult and specific sins which may have led to them being demonised. It will also include forgiveness of anyone against whom they hold resentment and may include confession of anger against God. Remember that anger held on to can cause a lodging place for the demonic, as we have already seen.

  It is also important to lead people to renounce any specific involvement in the occult, whether their own or that of their family. Renouncing is naming something as evil in the sight of God and confirming that we want nothing to do with it. It is not possible to repent of something of which we have not been personally guilty, but we can renounce any occult involvement in our family or among those who have influenced us. This includes renouncing any legalistic religion or cult involvement, and renouncing any addiction to drugs, alcohol or nicotine, if appropriate. Where people have occult books or objects in their possession, they must agree at this point to destroy them. Incidentally, it is important that they destroy these things themselves. You may go with them to give moral support and see that they go through with it, but do not take the responsibility for them of destroying such material. It is clear in Scripture that those who had been involved in occult activity burnt their occult materials themselves (Acts 19:19).

- We then need to release the person in Jesus' name from any curses and from family control, if the person has been under such control and if the family has been involved in the occult or has a history of sexual sin.

- We then command the spirit(s) to go in Jesus' name. It is important that we are creative and full of truth here. We do not just say, 'Go in Jesus' name... In Jesus' name, go.' We use truth from Scripture. We use the name of Jesus and all that it signifies, according to Philippians 2:6–11. We refer to the power of the blood of Jesus, the victory of Jesus over Satan, the power of the Holy Spirit, the truth of the empty cross and the empty tomb. We refer to the present position of Jesus as exalted above everything else. We also bring in the truth that the person is a new creation in Christ and their body is a temple of the Holy Spirit, and that therefore demons have no right to be there.

- It is important at this point not to raise the emotional temperature. If it seems to be taking time and a demon is not immediately going, then calm things down and chat with the person rather than just continually addressing the demon. It may be that there are footholds not yet dealt with. I take the view that if demons have not gone quickly, then there must be some reason for it and we need to discover what that is. We should be careful that we do not raise the emotional temperature ourselves. Demons are not deaf and though we speak to them authoritatively, a lot of shouting is not usually helpful.

- It is important to pray with our eyes open so that we can see what is going on. We need to listen to the Holy Spirit and seek discernment, but also to ask the person whether they feel the demon has gone. However, be wary of believing that it has gone, because if you are not easy in your spirit, the demon may be hiding. In that case, command it to reveal itself to you and then to go.

- If a demon manifests in a particular part of the body, it may be helpful, if appropriate, to lay hands there, or have somebody of the same sex lay hands there, and/or dedicate that area of the body to the Lord.

- Keep control of the person's eyes if you can, by maintaining eye contact. Sometimes you can see the demon manifesting itself behind the eyes.

- There is often controversy about the 'naming' of spirits. Some teach that it is necessary to obtain the demon's name before we have the authority to tell it to go. It is true that the Bible does name certain spirits – e.g. lying spirit, deaf and dumb spirit, spirit of fear, unclean spirit – but whether it is actually their 'name' or simply an identification of what those evil spirits are particularly doing to the person is unclear.

I have often found in practice that to show that you have uncovered what the evil spirit is doing has been helpful in causing it to manifest and go. Remember the word 'occult' means 'hidden'. Identifying the demon's activity is more important, however, for the person concerned than for us as we cast it out. It will help them to combat in the future any recurrence of the feelings that were caused by that evil spirit. If, for example, it is a spirit of rejection, then knowing that they have been set free from such a spirit helps them in their discipleship to learn how to handle any rejection in the future, without giving way to the intensity of feeling and anger that the evil spirit would have produced. However, it is important that we ourselves do not come into bondage to a particular method here, and assume that it is essential for us to know a demon's name. Evil spirits have to go in the name of Jesus, whether we know their 'name' or not.

● What about manifestations? These are the various ways in which a demon is showing that it is present and affecting the person, usually physically. Such manifestations can take various forms and we need to distinguish between two main types. There are those that occur when the demon leaves the person, and this might involve coughing or hard blowing, symptoms of vomiting or screaming. All these are manifestations of ejection and should not be stopped – or at least not immediately. There are other more showy examples of manifestations, e.g. sliding around the floor like a snake, or shaking violently or rolling around. These are just for show and we should not encourage them. If they occur, tell the demon to stop.

● It is important to encourage the person we are praying with to command the demon to go as well. It is helpful for them to say that they do not want to be under its authority any more and it should therefore leave them.

- If you really do not get through, do not worry. Pray for the person and fix another time, perhaps having prayed further or sought advice. There could be all sorts of reasons for this. If there is sin they are unwilling to confess and repent of, then we cannot proceed further. The issue here is that we want to help Christians grow in their faith and not just get rid of demons in their lives.

6 Aftercare

a) Aftercare is very, very important, especially in cases of severe demonisation. In these circumstances I believe you should meet with the person regularly, or ensure as best you can that someone else does so. It is important to build them up, encourage them and stand with them to resist the attacks of the devil. They should be encouraged in:

- worship;
- fellowship with others – the enemy often seeks to isolate us in such circumstances;
- building up in the word of God, particularly scriptures relevant to their situation.

b) Demons do try to get back. This is made clear in Luke 11:24–26. I believe they can regain entry if:

- the person persists in sin;
- they allow bitterness and unforgiveness to come into their lives once more;
- they are not in close Christian fellowship and being helped and prayed for to walk free.

c) Walking free. This is as important as the deliverance from evil spirits itself. It is the person taking responsibility for their own life, to walk free of sin and to renew their minds. Sometimes people to whom we are ministering have become passive and just allow things to happen to them. It is important that they are encouraged to take authority themselves over evil and live a godly life.

7 Backlash

We do sometimes experience the backlash of attacks upon ourselves, or our families, when we are engaged in such ministry. We must not fear it. We must encourage others to pray protection over us when we are particularly strongly involved in this ministry. We need to submit to God and resist the devil. This means that we will continue to do the work of God and persist against the devil's territory.

Practical Implementation

1 Introduction

This final seminar suggests ways in which all that has been taught in this course may be implemented in local churches. We recognise that different churches have different structures and therefore it is important that the principles laid out in this seminar are considered as helpful principles, rather than as a set blueprint for exactly how we should function.

As Christians, we long to see more of the dynamic healing power of God demonstrated in our personal lives and in our churches. As we have seen in Seminar 1, it is important that the counselling and healing ministry taught in this course is not separated from disciple-making, which is the responsibility of us all within our local churches. For most of us, the two main contexts in which we are likely to engage in prayer to set people free are a) prayer ministry in our services and meetings, and b) individuals or small teams of people meeting regularly with somebody to 'soak' their situation in prayer. Both need handling with wisdom and sensitivity.

Within this area of ministry, I believe there are different callings or different levels of involvement. Some may be called to general care, which could include ensuring that their friends receive further biblical counselling or prayer ministry, but not involve them taking part in such ministry themselves. Others will pray for the sick from time to time, perhaps after a service or with a friend. Yet others, however, will have it as one of their main functions within the local church. It is important that those who are regularly involved in praying for others in this way have attended an appropriate course and have been released to minister in this way by those with spiritual authority within the church.

2 Prayer ministry during and after services

Only in extreme circumstances should it be necessary to go out during a service for ministry. This would normally only be recommended if the person manifesting the problem is causing a disturbance to others and therefore detracting from what God is doing generally. It is normally better to let God deal with the person where they are during the service. Let them stay in the presence of God, even if they are weeping or God is dealing with them in some other way.

It is important that prayer should be available for one another in all our gatherings together, even though there may not always be specific ministry times.

Because of the importance of the whole body functioning, we should encourage all to feel free to minister to one another in our meetings unless there is a specific reason why somebody should not do so. In that case, they need to be told not to get involved. However, it is important that leaders and others with experience notice what is going on and intervene if necessary. Obviously as a church gets a lot bigger this may not be possible, and it may be necessary to have a specific ministry team. It is also important to have such a ministry team on occasions where a number of churches are getting together and therefore do not know one another so well, or in major evangelistic meetings when a lot of people from outside the church may be present.

At Stoneleigh Bible Weeks, we gave a summary of our training guidelines for public ministry. These are attached as an appendix since they may be helpful to others.

3 Ministry teams

As we have said, there are various ways in which prayer ministry can be organised within the church. Churches that have a strong cell system may well encourage healing prayer to take place in the context of these cell groups whenever possible and practical. However, it is also often helpful that those who have a major ministry or expertise in this area are available to supplement the cell groups, otherwise cell group leaders may become overwhelmed if there are a number of people with severe problems in their group. There may well be a ministry leader within the church for this particular purpose, and the cell group leaders should consult with that leader in order to bring in the relevant expertise if the cell group cannot handle any particular situation.

a) General principles

i) Accountability and oversight. Though there may well be situations where one-to-one biblical counselling is appropriate, the principles set out in this course are generally better undertaken by teams. These would normally be teams of two or three people who are ministering to a particular person. If such teams are operating within a cell group, they need to be accountable to the cell group leader(s) who are in turn accountable to the pastors or elders of the church. It is very important to be under authority if we are exercising authority, and such oversight is vital if healing prayer teams are to function effectively as part of the ministry of the whole church. The object of such oversight is to care for, protect, support and equip you in this ministry.

ii) Leadership. It is important that each team has a clear leader and that everyone on the team knows who the leader is. This creates security both within the team and for the person being ministered to, who is therefore more likely to open up to God. This does not mean that the leader needs to dominate each session and, within a session, leadership may be handed over to somebody else. However, it is the decision of the leader as to whether or not to do this.

iii) Goals and reviews. Sometimes counselling and prayer ministry can continue interminably and can become a substitute for friendship and normal relationships within the church. It is important not to keep on meeting for the sake of meeting as this can easily create dependency. On the other hand, we still want to give people ample time to apply the word of God in their lives and help them towards Christian freedom. Therefore, at the initial meeting, it is

good to specify how many sessions you are going to meet
for and set up a team accordingly. It is important to have a
review after that period of time. I would question the value
of going beyond six sessions without a review time, but I do
not believe either that it is right to stop just because the six
sessions are up, if the problems have clearly not been
overcome. At review times examples of questions that could
be asked are:

- What has been achieved so far?
- Is the person living in the good of what has been
  ministered so far?
- Is there any evidence of changed lifestyle? Has there
  been slipping back?
- What areas still need looking at?

It may be appropriate then either to arrange further sessions
or to take a break for a few weeks. A break will give an
opportunity to ascertain whether ground covered is being
'stood on' by the person receiving ministry and whether or
not they are 'walking free'. Sometimes there are lots of
issues to be discussed and prayed about and therefore
setting goals for future sessions can create a helpful focus.
However, it is important that there is flexibility. We need to
come under the guidance of the Holy Spirit and not be so
goal-oriented that we fail to open ourselves up to the Holy
Spirit's direction.

b) A few practical hints

i) Note-taking. Sometimes notes do need to be taken,
    otherwise it can be rather confusing and we can forget what
    has been said. However, it is important to talk about this
    first of all to the person being counselled and receiving
    prayer. Sometimes it is helpful to agree those notes with the
    person concerned. Such notes need to be kept confidential
    and in a secure place. It is also important to decide what
    will happen to the notes when prayer and counselling is
    finished. They are usually given to the person receiving
    prayer or ripped up if that is more appropriate.

ii) It is helpful to find a quiet place for counselling and ministry. It is best without the disruption of children.

iii) It is good for the team to meet to pray together prior to counselling and ministering to somebody.

iv) It is important that we encourage the person being counselled to develop ordinary social relationships. This must include opportunities for the team themselves to get to know the person and to be able to ask questions about their life, thus showing an interest in them beyond simply the matters for which counselling is taking place. Otherwise we just focus on problems and this can lead to what is called 'navel-gazing'.

v) Relationships with other agencies e.g. doctors, social services. Sometimes doctors or those in social services will talk to a 'minister' in a professional capacity but would not recognise people on a ministry team except as friends of the person receiving help – which, of course, hopefully they are! It can often be very helpful for consultation to take place between a 'minister' and these agencies. In order to do this, however, the permission of the person being counselled is required. Such permission will need to be given both to the church minister – normally a full-time pastor or elder – and to the doctor or social worker.

vi) If a person is not a committed member of the church in which the team is set up, their own church leadership must be consulted before any ministry commences.

vii) Situations may arise where a problem is so personal that people in your own church need to receive counsel in another church. This can be discussed and arranged. It is not only a question of confidentiality, but of the person finding it awkward to keep meeting in church the people who have been helping them with a problem they are very embarrassed about. It also applies when there may not be the relevant expertise in a particular church.

4 Dangers in this ministry

a) The person who 'clings'

Many people fear their lives being overwhelmed by particular needy people. We recognise that we need to be compassionate but some are so needy that their problems can become overwhelming. In this connection we need to distinguish between i) a problem person and ii) a person with severe problems. What are the differences?

i) A problem person. A 'problem person' does not really want to be different. They have become so identified with their problems that they would rather keep them and see that as a focus and basis on which others can relate to them.

    They rarely put into practice anything that is suggested but come back next time with a different problem. They also often go around to different people with different stories. There is still a basic need for repentance, which we covered in Seminar 2.

    At first such people may be very accusatory of others whom they allege should have helped them but have not. For example, they may have come from another church. It can sometimes be very flattering to hear that your church is so different from the church down the road, that you 'really help people'. Nevertheless, be careful and check with the church from which they have come. A year or so later you may find the same complaints are alleged about you and your church!

    However, we must still see such a 'problem person' as made in the image of God. We must approach them with a heart of compassion but nevertheless with firmness, because we recognise what their real need is. We want to help them towards repentance.

ii) A person with severe problems. These people are very grateful for the time you spend with them. They try to put advice into practice even though they may frequently fall and fail. They will be loyal to those helping them.

Sometimes it is difficult to tell the difference at first between these two types of people, each of which may appear very demanding. However, in either case, both firmness and compassion are needed. It is important that we never start off by assuming that people are in the first category. It is better to assume they are in the second until proved otherwise. Be guided by those 'over you in the Lord', those who are supervising your counselling ministry in these circumstances, and make sure that the ministry team itself remains united, otherwise it could be open to manipulation.

More generally, the following are important:

- Always preserve times of privacy. We cannot be helping others all the time – we need times with our families and close friends, and times on our own. Sometimes it can appear almost rude to say 'no' to someone in need, but we must be firm in protecting our own well-being. However, do not be so legalistic about your times of privacy that you become inflexible and effectively unable to serve.

- Try to fix times for counselling and ministry when it is convenient to you. However, also recognise that there will be emergencies from time to time and that compassion and some sacrifice of convenience are called for in such circumstances.

- People with very real difficulties need teaching to develop general friendships within the church as well as with you. Sometimes we can be involved with ministering to and counselling our friends and then such help blurs and distorts our friendship relationship so that the person can become dependent on prayer ministry.

- Sometimes this ministry can appear a bit risky. For example, people may threaten suicide. This is a difficult area and you should always take counsel from those who are supervising you. Certainly the first time it is important always to respond to such a threat. However, we do need to be aware that such a 'cry for help' can become a manipulative tool. The fact that we are serving and counselling somebody does not mean that we become totally responsible for them.

- We always need to examine our motives. If we are saying 'no' to further time with somebody, we need to ensure that our motives are genuinely for their good and the good of our own personal and family life and walk with God. We need to be careful that we do not say 'no' simply because 'we don't feel like it', or even out of class or racial prejudice. Sometimes it can seem more fulfilling to minister to those we naturally find attractive or who come from the same background as ourselves. We need to guard against this attitude. When He was on earth, Jesus touched and mixed with all kinds of people whom others despised, including prostitutes, tax collectors, lepers, a Samaritan woman and other outcasts. We need to ensure that our attitude is Christlike if we are involved in this sort of service for God.

b) Emotional dependency

Those we are helping can develop an emotional dependency on us as counsellors and helpers. We need to recognise it and talk it through with somebody overseeing us, who has pastoral responsibility. Sometimes it also has to be discussed with the person concerned in order to help them to freedom. We must be careful that we do not fall for flattery – we all like being needed. Sometimes the person we are helping may become jealous or possessive, and we can feel that we are being restricted from making friends with others in need. We must not be bound by people's dependency upon us. We need to keep walking free from it. This may cause problems, but worse problems are caused long term by an emotionally dependent relationship.

We can even become emotionally dependent ourselves. We can get so wrapped up in the other person's need and so keen that they come through to freedom, that if they fail to respond to godly counsel, we can become hurt ourselves. We need to keep this ministry in perspective. Our security must be in God, we must have broad friendships within the body of Christ and we must guard against having our security in our own ministry or in those we are helping. We have to leave the results to God and to the relationship that each person has with Him. It is even possible for us to go in for this sort of counselling within the body of Christ because it meets our own needs in some way. We must watch out for this and ensure that this does not become our motivation (see below).

We particularly need to be alert to the danger of emotional dependency across the sexes – women to men, or men to women. Sometimes it is helpful to have on a counselling team somebody of the opposite sex to the person being counselled. However, as I have stressed before, it is important that there is always somebody present of the same sex as the person being counselled.

c) Manipulation

i) Some people will try to manipulate us, and we have referred to this a number of times already. People will say things like, 'Of course, if you really cared...' or 'I understand you cannot come. I'm just not sure I'll manage if you don't' or 'I've never been able to trust anyone before and now you seem to be letting me down'. This last statement can be made when you are confronting somebody with truth to which they do not wish to respond positively.

ii) There can also be manipulation on our part. Those of us engaged in counselling ministry can start controlling people with guilt so that they feel the need to take steps to freedom that they are not yet ready or willing to take. They do it to please us. We must be prepared to let people go, and beware of any wrong sense of urgency on our part. People need to take responsibility for their own lives and decisions, and manipulating somebody to 'freedom' will not bear fruit in the long term.

It is also possible to use our pastoral authority wrongly and constantly remind the individual of our position and their rebellion. This does not give them space to respond to the word of God. We may be tempted towards this abuse of authority when we are frustrated in the place of prayer and a clear explanation of the truth has not produced the changes we hoped for.

d) Ministry replacing friendship

Our relationships with needy people can become problem-oriented, so that all we talk about is their problems. This is not only unhealthy, but counter-productive, since many problems in people's lives are actually overcome simply through genuine friendship and acceptance rather than through counselling and prayer ministry. Sometimes, indeed, part of the problem is that the person does not have genuine friendships and ensuring that they learn to make and keep friends is as important as prayer and counsel.

e) Not every problem in people's lives is solved by counselling and prayer ministry

Often what is required is obedience, repentance, and a clear understanding and knowledge of God's work.

We can also be in great danger of blaming every quirk of character on things that happened in our childhood. We need rather to enjoy our different personalities, contributions and even our varied histories. These are not an accident with God. We also need to watch the danger of people avoiding responsibility for their sins. We can find too that people who get involved in this sort of service can be in danger of a constant amateur psychoanalysis of themselves and others. This is not what we are about. We are here to apply the word of God prayerfully and lovingly to people's lives.

f) Ministering out of our own needs

We can have an unhealthy passion to know about people's lives that is nothing better than plain, old-fashioned nosiness, in which we ask questions not so much to help people as to satisfy our own curiosity. We need to check our motives honestly before God.

This sort of ministry, in particular, can be undertaken in order to gain acceptance.

It can also be that we have the same problems ourselves that we are trying to help others to get free from. I have sometimes seen a self-satisfied smirk on a person's face when they find that somebody else has a problem just like theirs! There can be a mutual joining together of inappropriate sympathy instead of helping each other to apply the word of God to our lives and thus come to genuine Christian freedom.

5 The cost of this ministry

It is costly to help one another. David says, 'I will not sacrifice to the Lord my God burnt offerings that cost me nothing' (2 Samuel 24:24). It is the command of Jesus that we love one another and care for one another (John 13:34). We therefore need to do so, whether we feel like it that day or not.

It is important for us to carry on even when things get tough in our own circumstances. Sometimes we ourselves can suffer the enemy's counter-attack. Our own marriage can start being affected by the same things that we are counselling somebody else about in their marriage. In these cases we need to submit to God and resist the devil.

It is important that we are able to receive counsel, prayer ministry and correction, as well as give it.

However, to engage in helping people to freedom is worth it. It brings blessing to them, to the church, to the extension of the kingdom of God and to our own lives and families. Remember that the whole purpose of bringing Christian counsel and sympathy is to make people more effective in their Christian service and thus extend the kingdom of God. We are not there just to make people 'feel better'. We want every soldier to be engaged in the battle.

Guidelines for Ministry Teams

Practical matters

- Always submit to your own church team leader, or to any elder or other team leader who directs you.

- Each meeting you will be allocated to a particular block. Seats will be reserved for you at the front of the block with one or two exceptions. You should check with your team leader on arrival in case there are specific instructions concerning that particular meeting. He will have just attended a briefing meeting.

- If for any reason you cannot attend the meeting or intend to swap with another team member (if your church is operating a rota system), then please ensure your team leader is aware of the change.

- Only those with 'Ministry Team' badges will be allowed to pray with people, so *please ensure you wear your badge at all times during ministry.* (NB Please carry your badge with you when not 'on duty' in case you are called upon to help.) Particularly, be available to minister at seminars if required. Please *wear your badge high up* where it can be easily seen by those overseeing ministry – it is not easy to see when it is at the bottom of your jeans or jumper!

- Where relevant, directions for ministry times will be given from the platform. On most occasions, you will pray for people in the aisles. Ensure that there is sufficient room for ministry and don't remove chairs to create space (fire regulations).

Ministering to others

Respecting the individual and helping them feel comfortable

- Before praying, just ask for their name. Later, it may be helpful to ask what is happening.

- Remember personal hygiene. People won't be blessed if you've got BO or have just eaten garlic! Try sucking mints before a ministry time.

- Women on the ministry team must be discreet about what they wear.

- If the person has fallen and they are of a different sex to you, do not bend over them. Let a person of the same sex do that if necessary.

- Avoid counselling. This should be done in a local church context. If you feel that someone needs specialist help during the Bible Week, mention this to your team leader.

- Avoid 'heaviness' or 'intensity'.

- Always retain the dignity of the individual, including confidentiality (though you must feel free to call in your team leader if what is shared with you is 'out of your depth').

- The person you are praying with needs to be assured that they are the most important person at that moment, so don't let your mind and eyes wander onto other situations in the room.

Praying for people to be baptised in the Holy Spirit

- As God moves in His Spirit in various other ways, we must not neglect this essential foundational truth: we believe there could well be people who experience a touch of the Holy Spirit without necessarily receiving the baptism in the Holy Spirit and the power, assurance of God's love and ability to move in spiritual gifts that baptism in the Holy Spirit brings. Please follow the guidelines given to you by your ministry team leader prior to Stoneleigh.

When God moves sovereignly

Let Him do so without getting involved, unless a disturbance is being caused or a person is particularly distressed. Even then, be careful not to 'comfort' if what is actually happening is conviction of sin intended to lead to repentance.

Sensitivity to the Holy Spirit

- Remember what the Spirit has been saying through the ministry of the word and keep focused on Christ.

- Watch what the Holy Spirit is doing. If nothing appears to be happening, speak loving words, encourage them to 'soak' and move on. You could return later.

- Don't pressure yourself or the one you are praying for. Watch the amount of your words, relax and let the Holy Spirit do His work.

- Don't be too subjective but do share the scriptures God brings to mind. If you have a prophetic word (particularly of a directive nature), involve your team leader so that it can be weighed. Be clear when giving the word that the person is free not to take it on board if it does not strike a chord with them. Encourage them to share it with their elder for weighing.

- If people go down in the Spirit, continue to pray for them, inviting the Holy Spirit to continue ministering to them. Be careful not to interrupt when you discern there is a special 'conversation' going on between the person and the Lord.

Prayer engagement

- Pray in pairs, ensuring someone is available to 'catch'. (On the rare occasion you find yourself having to pray for someone alone, only pray with the same sex.)

- The person catching need not necessarily be a member of the ministry team if there are so many people requiring prayer that others are asked to catch. However, non-badged people should not be allowed to get further involved in the prayer ministry.

- If the person has fallen and they are of a different sex, do not bend down over them; let a person of the same sex do that if necessary. The same applies to giving comfort, e.g. putting an arm around someone if they are distressed.

- If you feel unable to deal with a situation (e.g. deliverance), don't press on regardless. Seek help from your ministry team leader. He will have access to those who can minister in specialist areas, if necessary.

- If your hand or body begins shaking, pray with your hands slightly away from the person so as not to distract them.

- If you're a 'catcher', put your hands lightly in the small of the person's back to give confidence.

PERSONAL NOTES